AIR CAMPAIGN

THE OIL CAMPAIGN 1944–45

Draining the Wehrmacht's lifeblood

T0322678

STEVEN J. ZALOGA | ILLUSTRATED BY EDOUARD A. GROULT

OSPREY PUBLISHING
Bloomsbury Publishing Plc
Kemp House, Chawley Park, Cumnor Hill, Oxford OX2 9PH, UK
29 Earlsfort Terrace, Dublin 2, Ireland
1385 Broadway, 5th Floor, New York, NY 10018, USA
E-mail: info@ospreypublishing.com
www.ospreypublishing.com

OSPREY is a trademark of Osprey Publishing Ltd

First published in Great Britain in 2022

A catalogue record for this book is available from the British Library.

ISBN: PB 9781472848543; eBook: 9781472848550;
ePDF: 9781472848574; XML: 9781472848567

22 23 24 25 26 10 9 8 7 6 5 4 3 2 1

Maps by www.bounford.com
Diagrams by Adam Tooby
3D BEVs by Paul Kime
Index by Angela Hall
Typeset by PDQ Digital Media Solutions, Bungay, UK
Printed and bound in India by Replika Press Private Ltd.

To find out more about our authors and books visit www.ospreypublishing.com. Here you will find extracts, author interviews, details of forthcoming events, and the option to sign up for our newsletter.

Glossary

AWM	Australian War Memorial
CBO	Combined Bomber Offensive
CCS	Combined Chiefs of Staff
Flak Flugabwehrkanone	Anti-aircraft gun
Geschwader	Luftwaffe Wing, composed of 3–4 *Gruppen*; 120–160 fighters
Gruppe	Group, consisting of 3 *Staffelen* and *Stab*, 40 fighters
JäFu Jagdfliegerführer	Fighter control
JG Jagdgeschwader	German fighter squadron
LAC	Library and Archive Canada
NJG Nachtjagdgeschwader	German night-fighter squadron
RAAF	Royal Australian Air Force
RCAF	Royal Canadian Air Force
Stab	Luftwaffe Staff, headquarters
Staffel	Luftwaffe squadron, 10 fighters
Ton	Short ton (2,000lbs)
Tonne	Metric ton (2,204lbs)
USSTAF	US Strategic Air Forces in Europe

Author's Note:
Luftwaffe wings (*Geschwader*) were identified by a numerical suffix, for example, JG 27. Within the Geschwader, the three or four Gruppen were identified by Roman numbers, for example II./JG 27. The smaller Staffel were identified by an Arabic numeral, for example 5./JG 27.

Unless otherwise noted, all photos in this book are from US government sources including the National Archives and Records Administration II at College Park, Maryland, and the Library of Congress in Washington, DC.

CONTENTS

INTRODUCTION 4

CHRONOLOGY 6

ATTACKER'S CAPABILITIES 7

DEFENDER'S CAPABILITIES 13

CAMPAIGN OBJECTIVES 25

THE CAMPAIGN 31

ANALYSIS 89

FURTHER READING 93

INDEX 95

INTRODUCTION

The Oil Campaign was the most decisive Allied air operation of World War II. Started in May 1944, the campaign aimed to destroy the German fuel industry. The campaign was delayed due to the commitments of the Allied heavy bomber forces to missions supporting the forthcoming Operation *Overlord* invasion, as well as the diversion of missions to attack German V-Weapon sites as part of Operation *Crossbow*.

The Oil Campaign was executed by three principal elements. The US Army Air Forces contributed two of these, the Eighth Air Force, operating out of Britain, and the Fifteenth Air Force operating out of Italy. The Royal Air Force employed Bomber Command from bases in Britain, though there was also a small RAF contingent with Fifteenth Air Force in Italy.

The Oil Campaign was primarily the initiative of Gen. Carl Spaatz, commander of US Strategic Air Forces in Europe. The short-term goal was to cut off the Luftwaffe's high-octane aircraft fuel. Air Marshal Arthur "Bomber" Harris was unenthusiastic about the plan, calling the German oil industry a "panacea target." After the first set of bombing missions in the spring of 1944, Allied intelligence intercepted and decrypted a string of German messages indicating that Berlin viewed the attacks on the synthetic fuel plants with considerable alarm. Eisenhower's deputy, Air Marshal Arthur Tedder, became a firm supporter of the Oil Plan, and in concert with Air Marshal Charles Portal of the British Air Ministry, put pressure on Harris to participate in the campaign starting in the summer of 1944.

The initial Eighth Air Force raids against the large synthetic fuel plants had an immediate and drastic effect on the German production of aviation fuel. Although many plants were put out of operation for weeks or months, previous attacks against the Romanian oil installations near Ploesti had made it clear that the plants had to be repeatedly attacked to overcome German repair efforts. As a result, the Oil Campaign was a long, attritional struggle lasting well into 1945.

The Germans reinforced the Flak defenses around the synthetic fuel plants, but to little avail. Although Flak continued to damage many Allied bombers and degrade the accuracy of the attacks, it was never effective enough to halt the bombing raids. The Luftwaffe day-fighter force inflicted heavier casualties than Flak, but average bomber loss rates were around 2 percent in late 1944 and only 1 percent in 1945. In contrast, the Luftwaffe continued to suffer from a lack of skilled pilots, in no small measure due to fuel shortages. As a result, in the aerial battles over Germany, the Luftwaffe day-fighters suffered disproportionate losses against the USAAF escort fighters, often losing a quarter of their fighters during many large engagements.

The Luftwaffe hoped to shift the technological balance in the daylight missions by the introduction of new rocket and jet fighters. The first Me 163 rocket fighters were assigned to defend the largest of the German oil facilities, the massive Leuna works. Ultimately, the Me 163 had little effect on the balance of airpower due to its dangerous propulsion system. The new Messerschmitt Me 262 was a far more formidable fighter aircraft, dangerous to bombers and escort fighters alike. However, it was available in very small numbers into 1945. It never reached its full potential. Its novel jet engines lacked durability, and it suffered from the same lack of skilled pilots as the rest of the Luftwaffe.

RAF Bomber Command took very heavy losses to Luftwaffe night-fighters in the initial oil missions in the summer of 1944. This was in part due to Luftwaffe advances in electronic warfare systems. By autumn, Bomber Command had instituted new tactics and equipment that reduced the loss rate to acceptable levels. Bomber Command initially focused its Oil Campaign missions on plants in the Ruhr industrial belt. In December 1944, the Air Ministry pressured Harris to extend missions to the large plants in eastern Germany since the US Eighth Air Force was preoccupied with missions connected to the Ardennes campaign.

The synthetic fuel industry was an integral part of the German chemical industry that also produced the key ingredients for rubber, high explosives and a wide range of other key industrial products. Destruction of the synthetic fuel industry caused substantial collateral damage to related chemical industries. The ultimate aim of the campaign was to "kill" the German Industrial Octopus." By early 1945, the Oil Campaign succeeded in drastically reducing German fuel stockpiles to the point where it curtailed Wehrmacht combat operations. Fuel shortages forced the Kriegsmarine to restrict nearly all operations except for some U-boat missions. Shortages of high-octane aviation fuel dramatically reduced the training time for Luftwaffe pilots to the point where new pilots were unprepared for combat missions. Shortages of motor fuel constrained army operations in all theaters. German leaders after the war noted that the fuel shortages were one of the reasons that the German army was unable to exploit its Panzer reserve to block the advance of the Red Army on the road to Berlin in January–February 1945.

By April 1945, the German oil industry had been pounded into rubble. In parallel to the Oil Plan, the Allied heavy bombers had also been engaging in a Transportation Plan that shattered the German railroad and industrial canal system. This cut the supply of coal that had been moving to factories. By the early spring of 1945, the German war industries were in a state of chaos and complete collapse.

CHRONOLOGY

1943

August 1 US Army Air Force conducts Operation *Tidal Wave* against the Romanian oil fields at Ploesti.

1944

April 1 Operation *Pointblank* ends; USSTAF falls under SHAEF command.

April 5 Fifteenth Air Force stages mission against Ploesti in the guise of a Transportation Plan mission.

April 20 Tedder approves first Oil Campaign mission in Germany.

May 12 Eighth Air Force stages its first Oil Campaign mission against a variety of German synthetic fuel plants.

May 15 Senior Luftwaffe officials meet to discuss possible antidotes against the threat to the fuel plants.

May 28 Eighth Air Force stages second main Oil Campaign mission, including attacks into Upper Silesia.

May 31 Edmund Geilenberg appointed to program to develop industrial techniques in response to the Oil Campaign.

June 6 Allied forces stage Operation *Neptune* landings in Normandy causing a temporary halt in Oil Campaign.

June 8 Spaatz assigns the Oil Campaign as the primary mission of the USSTAF.

June 12–13 Bomber Command stages first Oil Campaign mission against plants in the Ruhr.

June 18 Eighth Air Force conducts first major Oil Campaign mission since Operation *Neptune*.

July 13 RAF secures a radar-equipped Ju 88G-1 when it lands in Britain.

July 20 Eighth Air Force spots a Me 163 rocket fighter for the first time.

July 25 Combat debut of Me 262 jet fighter-bomber.

August 16 First major commitment of Me 163 rocket fighter over Leuna.

August 29 Red Army captures Ploesti oil plants.

October 7 First Oil Campaign mission to encounter Me 262 jet fighter.

December 16 German Autumn Mist offensive in Ardennes starts.

1945

January 1 Operation *Bodenplatte* attack on Allied airfields.

January 19 Göring rebuffs "mutiny" of the fighter pilots; Galland exiled.

January 30 Speer warns Hitler collapse of the German economy in "4–8 weeks."

February 9 Combat debut of second Me 262 fighter unit KG(J) 54.

March 3–4 Luftwaffe conducts Operation *Gisela* intruder missions against Bomber Command.

March 1–31 German aviation fuel production only 40 tonnes.

April 1–30 No German aviation fuel production.

April 7 Operation *Werwolf* ramming attacks against Eighth Air Force.

ATTACKER'S CAPABILITIES
Allied bomber strength in 1944

Royal air force

Under the command of Air Marshal Arthur "Bomber" Harris, the primary role of Bomber Command was the area bombardment of German cities in the hopes of crushing German morale and "de-housing" German industrial workers. Its arsenal gradually shifted from its 1939–42 force of twin-engined bombers to larger and more potent four-engine heavy bombers. The Avro Lancaster and Handley Page Halifax became the backbone of the force. In comparison to their USAAF counterparts, the British heavy bombers carried a heavier bomb load but less defensive armament since they conducted their missions at night. As of July 1944, the RAF Bomber Command deployed 1,462 heavy bombers, primarily the Lancaster and Halifax. The smaller Mosquito bomber was widely used for Pathfinder missions.

Lancaster (KB700) "Ruhr Express," the first of 430 Lancasters manufactured in Canada starting in 1943. This particular aircraft served in 405 and 419 Squadrons RCAF in 6 Group and completed 49 missions before being written off due to an accident on January 2, 1945.

By the summer of 1944, Bomber Command had deployed seven groups, consisting of ten or more squadrons each. The 6 Bomb Group was formed by the Royal Canadian Air Force. Two of the other groups had specialized roles. The 8 Bomb Group was the specialized Pathfinder Force (PFF) while 100 Group was the electronic countermeasures formation as further described below.

Night bombing required specialized tactical techniques that evolved continually over 1941–44 in a deadly interplay with German defenses. Early night bombing missions were extremely inaccurate due to the difficulty of identifying targets in the dark. The Butt Report of August 18, 1941 determined that only one in ten bombers reaching Germany's Ruhr industrial region flew within five miles of their target. Only about 1 percent of bombs carried on these sorties hit in the vicinity of the target. A number of tactical and technical solutions were developed to address these shortcomings.

Bomber Command began adopting electronic night navigation aids including Gee starting in 1942. These proved most effective when used by specialized crews and, in August 1942, each group had a squadron assigned as a Pathfinder. New and more precise aids were gradually introduced, such as the Oboe in late 1942. In addition, specialized Pathfinder

A RCAF Halifax Mk. V (JD114) of 419 Squadron RCAF, 6 Group named "Medicine Hat" after the town in Alberta. This aircraft conducted over 50 missions. (LAC)

aircraft were also introduced, including modified Mosquito light bombers in early 1943. One of the most important RAF innovations was the introduction of the H2S terrain radar that saw its combat debut in February 1943.

In January 1943, the Pathfinders were consolidated into 8 Group rather than assigning one squadron per group. Eventually, 19 Pathfinder squadrons were raised. The ratio of Pathfinder bombers to the rest of the bombers in the Main Force was typically about 1-to-15, but higher ratios of Pathfinders could be employed depending on the mission.

The first wave of Pathfinders, dubbed the "Finders," dropped illuminating flares in a stream on the approaches to the target to aid the navigation of the Main Force. These were followed by "Illuminators" carrying the Target Indicator (TI) flares that were used to mark the target for the Main Force. The "Illuminators" were sometimes followed by "Markers"

A Mosquito FB VI (NT137 code TH-T) named "Lady Luck" of the 418 Squadron RCAF. This unit was assigned to a variety of missions including intruder missions against German night-fighters. It ended the war as the highest-scoring Canadian squadron. (LAC)

that would drop additional Target Indicators over the objective to refresh the first salvos of Target Indicators, after the first wave had burned out.

Bomber Command eventually adopted the technique of assigning an experienced commander to serve as a "Master Bomber." His aircraft would circle the target area and provide instructions to the Pathfinders and Main Force depending on the circumstances of the raid.

The 100 Group was formed in November 1943 to deal with the threat of German radar-directed weapons including radar-equipped night-fighters and radar-directed Flak guns. Mosquito night-fighters were equipped with electronic support measures that could detect the radar emissions of German night-fighters. Once identified, the Mosquitos could then use their own airborne radars to locate and attack the German night-fighters.

German Flak batteries were increasingly dependent on radars to warn of the approach of RAF bombers as well as to direct the fire of the guns. The RAF began using "Window" in July 1943. This consisted of metallized strips dropped in large volume to create a reflective cloud that blinded the German radar. Besides the use of Window, the 100 Group deployed a variety of electronic countermeasures, especially radar jammers, to further disrupt German defenses. The 100 Group also used communication jammers that interfered with the radio communications of the German ground control intercept (GCI) systems that directed the German night-fighters to their target.

A "Wizard War" evolved week-by-week as British and German electronic warfare engineers introduced new technology to defeat electronic countermeasures. In turn, new countermeasures were quickly adapted to address any innovations by the opposing side. In general, British electronic warfare tactics maintained an edge over German technology by the spring and summer of 1944 when the Oil Campaign began, though there were some important exceptions.

One of the most important and seldom recognized aspects of Britain's efforts in the Combined Bomber Offensive was a vigorous economic intelligence effort. This involved the collection of information on the organization and location of key German industries.

A B-17F-30-DL "Chennault's Pappy" (42-3172 OR-X) of the 323rd Squadron, 91st Bomb Group seen here being bombed up at RAF Bassingbourn on April 9, 1944 for Mission 293 by the 1st Bomb Division against Rahmel and Marienburg. These early B-17s were generally replaced by the summer of 1944 with the later B-17G fitted with nose turrets to defend against German fighter frontal attacks.

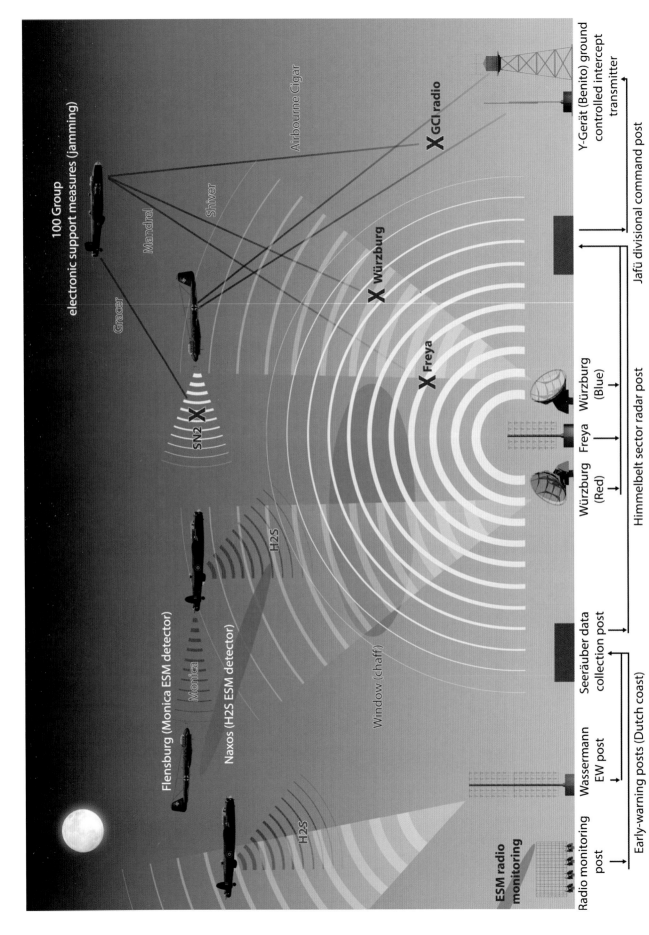

This information was essential for targeting. This data was collected by a variety of means including espionage, aerial reconnaissance, and electronic surveillance.

The destruction of much of the German fighter force by the summer of 1944 permitted Bomber Command to switch increasingly to daylight missions, By November 1944, Bomber Command conducted more daylight missions than night missions.

US Army Air Forces

The US Army Air Forces' air doctrine was heavily focused on the use of daylight heavy bombing to destroy the enemy's military industries. The USAAF bomber force in Europe did not reach a critical mass until the autumn of 1943 with the deployment of the Eighth Air Force operating out of Britain and the Fifteenth Air Force operating out of Italy. These formed the United States Strategic Air Force (USSTAF).

Early bombing missions into Germany in August–October 1943, notably the Schweinfurt–Regensburg missions, were only marginally successful in the face of German fighter and Flak defenses, incurring unacceptable losses.[1] As a consequence, the USSTAF shifted its priorities to the destruction of the Luftwaffe fighter force, codenamed Operation *Pointblank*.[2] The first phase of this campaign, codenamed Operation *Argument*, was conducted from November 1943 to February 1944. The aim of this campaign was both the destruction of the German aviation plants as well as the attrition of the German fighter force.

During combat, the interior of the B-17 quickly became flooded with expended brass casings from the .50 cal waist machine guns. The gunners had to wear protective clothing due to the intense cold at high altitude, and frequently wore "flak aprons" as well.

The most significant lesson from this phase of the campaign was the need for long-range escort fighters to shield the heavy bombers from Luftwaffe fighters. With the widespread introduction of long-range fighters such as the P-47D Thunderbolt and P-51D Mustang, the tide turned in favor of the daylight bomber force. This was made possible both through improvements in the fighters as well as the introduction of other innovations such as the use of drop-tanks to extend the range of the fighters. The escort fighters were largely successful in ending the threat of German rocket-firing heavy fighters and forced the Germans to switch to massed attacks using single-engine fighters.

The Eighth Air Force changed tactics in early 1944, freeing the escort fighters from close bomber escort, and permitting the fighters to

1   Marshall L. Michel, *Schweinfurt–Regensburg 1943: Eighth Air Force's costly early daylight battles* (Air Campaign 14), Osprey, 2020.

2   Steven Zaloga, *Operation Pointblank 1944: Defeating the Luftwaffe* (Campaign 230), Osprey, 2011.

ABOVE LEFT
A colorfully marked B-24H (42-94953) named "Rugged but Right" of the 712th Squadron, 448th Bomb Group, 2nd Division, returning to its base in Seething, England on March 12, 1945 following Mission 883 to Swinemünde on the Baltic coast.

ABOVE RIGHT
P-47D (44-1956, code MX-X) with the 82nd Squadron, 78th Fighter Group at Duxford in June 1944 shortly after it was painted with invasion stripes. The aircraft was named "Iron Ass" when flown by Lt.Col. Jack Oberhansly (5 victories) and "No Guts, No Glory" when flown by Lt. Col. Ben Mayo (4 victories).

chase down German fighters. This significantly increased German fighter attrition, a major aim of the *Pointblank* campaign. The US fighters had a number of advantages over their Luftwaffe opponents. German fighter pilot training decreased during 1943–44 and the American pilots were better trained. German fighter pilot training fell from about 160 hours in early 1944 to less than 120 hours in late 1944; USAAF fighter pilot training increased from over 300 hours to about 400 hours in the same period. In addition, the adaptation of the Bf 109 and Fw 190 to the anti-bomber mission led to the addition of external gun packs and other features that degraded their performance in the fighter-vs.-fighter role.

The USSTAF benefited from British innovations in navigation aids, and the US formations gradually adopted these systems, including the H2S radar as well as comparable US systems such as H2X (AN/APS-15). While these were not as necessary in daylight missions as in the RAF's night missions, they did enable attacks when cloud-cover or smoke obscured the target. As in the case of Bomber Command, the USTAAF made extensive use of "chaff," the American term for Window, to blind German air defense radars as well as other types of electronic countermeasures.

A P-51D of the 335th Squadron, 4th Fighter Group flown by Lt. Darwin L Berry based at Debden, England. This squadron was the offspring of 121 (Eagle) Squadron RAF of American volunteer pilots flying for the RAF prior to the American entry into the war.

DEFENDER'S CAPABILITIES
Luftflotte reich

Luftwaffe organization

The Reich defense command was Luftflotte Reich, based in Berlin. Through mid-1943, Reich air defense (*RLV: Reichluftverteidigung*) was based primarily on Flak and night-fighters since the main threat was RAF night attacks. Reich air defense started with a sophisticated network of electronic sensors to detect and track the approaching bombers. The first layer was positioned on the Dutch, Belgian, and French coasts, followed by additional posts into Germany. This sophisticated network was dubbed the Kammhuber Line by the Allies, named after its founder, Gen. Josef Kammhuber, but known to the Luftwaffe as the Himmelbelt system.

Several Ju 88G-6 night-fighters at Fliegerhorst Langensalza in April 1945. This airbase had been used by NJG 2 during 1944, but these are new production aircraft not yet issued to any unit.

Was Speer's 1944 fighter production program as successful as claimed? American analysts later concluded that the numbers had been inflated by double-counting fighters when they underwent modification. This Fw 190F-8 fighter-bomber (Werk Nr. 931884) started life as a Fw 190A-7 fighter (Werk Nr. 640069). Some fighters were found to have up to three different Werk Nummeren and so may have been counted three times. This aircraft served with Schlagtgeschwader 2 and is seen here preserved at the Udvar-Hazy Center of the US National Air and Space Museum.

OPPOSITE DEFENSE OF THE REICH FIGHTER UNITS (NOVEMBER 1944)

The *Luftnachricht Dienst* (Air Surveillance Service) provided the Luftwaffe's early warning and tracking units. In its most basic form, it consisted of visual observation posts (*Flugwache*). An electronic intelligence early warning service (*Funkaufklärungsdienst*) monitored the radio channels used by Allied bomber formations during the preparatory phases of the missions over England; by 1943 the system was expanded to include sensors such as Samos and Fano that monitored additional electronic emissions such as the bomber radars. The data was fed to the *Seeräuber* (Pirate) data collection center at Zeist in the Netherlands which supported the nearby I.Jagdkorps command post, codenamed *Diogenes*. Long-range search radars such as the Mammut and Wassermann types were deployed along the French, Belgian, and Dutch coasts. These picked up the Allied bombers as they crossed the Channel and then the targets were handed over to the belts of forward-alert radar centers with the smaller Freya and Würzburg radars which continued to track the bombers as they approached and entered German airspace. The surveillance and radar information was reported to a regional air warning center (*Fluko: Flugwachkommando*) and each Fluko in turn passed the data reported to its central divisional command post.

Major urban and industrial centers in Germany were protected by Flak units that had their own network of close-range tracking devices including acoustic listening posts, searchlights, and fire control radars. Although the acoustic posts and searchlights gradually gave way to radars in 1942–43, they saw a revival in late 1943–1944 when the Allies began using electronic-warfare tactics to jam the radars.

In 1944, the data from the various layers of sensors were fed to a *Jagdabschnittsführer* ("JaFü": Fighter Sector Director) established in February 1944 in the fighter division command centers. The busiest of these were the *Dädalus* command post in Deelen of 1.Jagddivision, and *Sokrates* in Stade of the 2.Jagddivision. The divisional command posts were highly sophisticated data collection and dissemination stations, derisively called "Battle opera houses" by the fighter pilots for their elaborately choreographed procedures. The radar and other data were collated and the air situation report created which was then used by the fighter director to assign missions to the division's various fighter units. The fighter units used this data as the basis for their ground-control-intercept (GCI) network.

Direction of the fighters was conducted by voice radio from the fighter control center (*Jägerleit Gefechtstand*) at the division command post. The key link between the ground-control-intercept system on the ground and the fighters in the air was the *Y-Vehrfahren-Kampf* (Y-Combat System), better known by its British codename, *Benito*. The system's FuS AN 733 ground stations interacted with a FuG16ZY transponder on the fighter which retransmitted the signal back to the ground, allowing the Y-Gerät to track friendly fighters. Not all fighters had this equipment, often a single fighter per Staffel.

The Luftwaffe's ground-control-intercept system came under increasing stress in the summer and autumn of 1943 due to the Allies introduction of radar countermeasures starting with the RAF use of Window in July 1943. One expedient method used to circumvent the growing electronic warfare threat was the use of Fühlungshalter "shadow" aircraft which flew alongside Allied bomber formations and reported their course, altitude, and direction. By late 1943, the Jagddivisionen each had at least one shadow unit, usually using Ju 88C heavy fighters.

The best of the German single-engine day-fighters in 1944 was the Fw 190D-9 introduced in the summer of 1944. In contrast to the previous Fw 190A series, it was powered by the Junkers Jumo 213A 12-cylinder engine, offering 1,775hp.

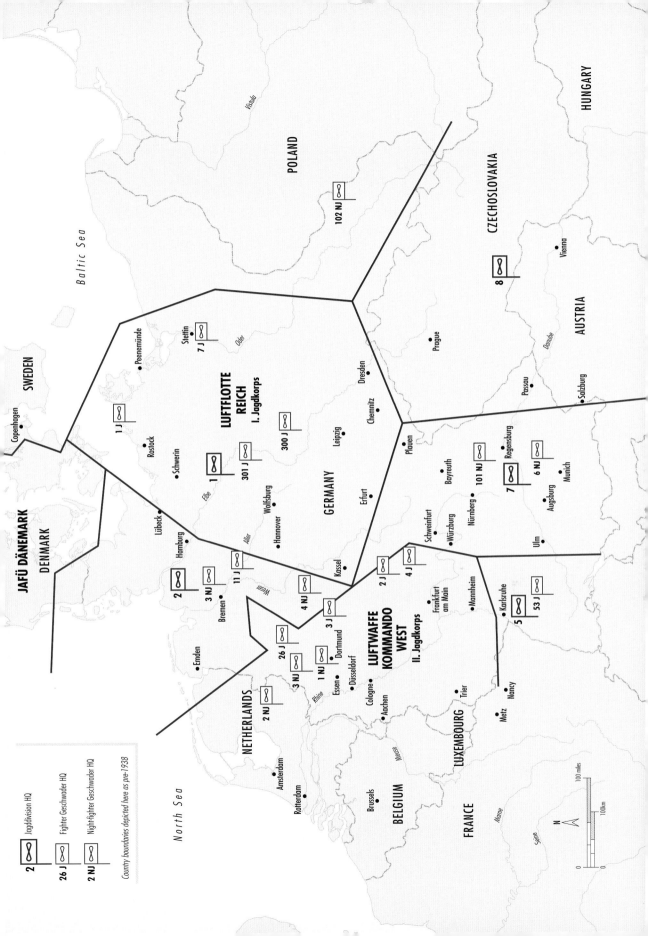

Country boundaries depicted here as pre-1938

Jagddivision HQ

Fighter Geschwader HQ

Night-fighter Geschwader HQ

2

26 J

2 NJ

North Sea

Baltic Sea

SWEDEN

Copenhagen

DENMARK

JAFÜ DÄNEMARK

NETHERLANDS

Amsterdam

Rotterdam

BELGIUM

Brussels

LUXEMBOURG

Trier

FRANCE

Metz

Nancy

Marne

Seine

Meuse

Emden

Bremen

Hamburg

Lübeck

Rostock

Schwerin

Peenemünde

Stettin

Oder

Elbe

Weser

Aller

Hannover

Wolfsburg

Kassel

Erfurt

Leipzig

Dresden

Chemnitz

Plauen

Bayreuth

Nürnberg

Würzburg

Schweinfurt

Frankfurt am Main

Mannheim

Karlsruhe

Augsburg

Munich

Ulm

Regensburg

GERMANY

LUFTFLOTTE REICH
I. Jagdkorps

LUFTWAFFE KOMMANDO WEST
II. Jagdkorps

Cologne

Aachen

Essen

Düsseldorf

Dortmund

Rhine

POLAND

Vistula

CZECHOSLOVAKIA

Prague

AUSTRIA

Vienna

Passau

Salzburg

Danube

HUNGARY

102 NJ

8

7 J

1 J

301 J

300 J

101 NJ

6 NJ

7

2

3 NJ

11 J

4 NJ

26 J

3 J

3 NJ

1 NJ

2 NJ

4 J

2 J

53 J

5

4 J

N

0   100km

0   100 miles

The Luftwaffe's ground-control-interception system was centered around the "Battle Opera Houses." This is a wartime artist's impression of the 3. Jagddivision's *Diogenes* command post at Deelen in the Netherlands in 1944. The division commander, his staff and associated liaison officers (1) sit above and behind the banks of *Jägerleitoffizieren* fighter direction officers who controlled the fighter squadrons by radio. The main situation map (2) kept track of the location and direction of approaching bomber formations (5,6,7). The main situation map was supported by a separate reference map group (8) which kept track of friendly fighters by means of the Y-Combat System. They passed this data to signals troops at the back of the room (3) who plotted the positions on the main map using light projectors, along with data from the threat tracking staff above (4).

The fighter elements of Luftflotte Reich were subordinated to I. Jagdkorps, located in the Cäser command post in Zeist in the Netherlands before being moved back to Braunschweig-Querum in the summer of 1944 and finally to Treuenbrietzen, near Berlin, in October 1944. The fighter force was organized on a regional basis under the control of a *Jagddivision* (Fighter Division). In the autumn of 1944, there were four of these involved in the defense of the Reich, supplemented by two more with Luftflotte 3 on the approaches to the Reich. These divisions were of mixed composition including both day and night-fighter Geschwaderen, and each division also controlled three or four Nachrichten Regimenten which operated the regional radar and sensor networks.

A fighter Geschwader was roughly equivalent to a RAF Wing or AAF Group and were classified by type: *Jagdgeschwader* (JG; day-fighter); *Zerstörerjagdgeschwader* (ZG: heavy fighter); and *Nachtjagdgeschwader*, (NJG: night-fighter). The Geschwader included three or four Gruppen. On paper, each Gruppe had 40 fighters, though operational strength was usually less. A Gruppe was in turn broken down into *Staffel* and then *Schwadron*. The divisions did not control a specific number or type of Geschwader, but were primarily command-and-control organizations with fighter units moved around by higher commands as the campaign warranted. As a result, the Gruppen of each Geschwader were not necessarily subordinated to a single division.

Through the summer of 1944, the tactical air forces on the invasion front were controlled independently by Luftflotte 3 based in Paris. Their fighter units were not directly assigned to the Reich defense mission, but they often intercepted Allied bomber formations attacking targets in France and the Low Countries. The collapse of the Wehrmacht in France and Belgium in August–September 1944 led to a substantial reorganization of the Luftwaffe in the west. Luftflotte 3 was redesignated *Luftwaffenkommando West* (Air Command West) on September 26, 1944 and remained in control of the tactical air units facing the Allied armies. These were engaged in their own air defense campaign since Allied tactical fighter and bomber units were based near the German frontier and were increasingly active over western Germany.

The tactical fighter units of Luftwaffenkommando West were controlled by II.Jagdkorps, headquartered at Flammersfeld near Koblenz.

LUFTWAFFE FIGHTER STRENGTH JUNE–DECEMBER 1944	30 Jun 44		30 Sep 44		31 Dec 44	
	On hand	Ready	On hand	Ready	On hand	Ready
Russian Front						
Single engine day	414	274	373	311	469	377
Twin engine day	18	15	100	88		
Twin engine night	118	78	187	169	102	81
Russian Front sub-total	550	367	660	568	571	458
Mediterranean Front						
Single engine day	125	85				
Twin engine day	22	20				
Mediterranean Front sub-total	147	105				
Defense of the Reich						
Single engine day	448	258	1,244	829	473	264
Jet & Rocket	10	6	46	36	110	34
Twin engine day	161	72			67	60
Twin engine night	549	383	830	687	1,140	829
Defense of the Reich sub-total	1,168	719	2,120	1,552	1,790	1187
Western Front						
Single engine day	526	271	307	219	1,208	842
Twin engine day	41	17	42	34	38	25
Twin engine night	136	83			12	7
Western Front sub-total	703	371	349	253	1,258	874
Total	2,568	1,562	3,129	2,373	3,619	2,519

The single-engine day-fighters available for Reich defense in early 1944 were mostly Bf 109G and Fw 190A tactical fighters. These had originally been designed for fighter-vs.-fighter combat and their original armament was not well suited to destroying heavy bombers. Their 13mm machine guns were almost useless against a B-17 and a German study concluded that on average it took twenty 20mm hits to shoot down a B-17. Since only about 2 percent of the rounds fired actually hit, this implied that it took 23 seconds of firing to down a B-17, an impossible duration under the circumstances, barring a few lucky hits. During 1943, a variety of 30mm cannon were added, most notably the powerful MK 108 30mm cannon on the Fw 190. A German study concluded that it only took three 30mm hits on average to down a B-17. Besides the internal MK 108 30mm cannon, new cannon were added under the wings of the single-engine fighters. The increasing firepower was evident in US reports which noted a ratio of 40 cannon hits per 100 machine gun hits in 1942, but 77 cannon hits per hundred machine gun hits by the first half of 1943. The rate of kills per engagement rose from 2.3 kills per hundred attacks in late 1942 to 3.6 by mid-1943, 5.0 by late 1943, and to a high of 17.7 by the spring of 1944. New fighter types were also introduced, notably the "long-nose" Fw 190D-9.

The inadequacies of the single-engine fighters led to increased use of twin-engine Zerstörer heavy fighters in the autumn of 1943 with the commitment of ZG 26 and ZG 76 to Reich defense. These two heavy fighter units were primarily equipped with the Bf 110G-2 and G-3, although ZG 26 also operated the Ju 88C-6. The new Me 410 began to be issued to these units in October 1943, eventually becoming a common type by the spring of 1944. The original 1943 tactics were to employ rockets from stand-off ranges to break up the bombers

One of the most common German radars used for ground-control intercept functions was the Telefunken FuMG.65 *Würzburg-Riese* (Giant Würzburg) radar. This one was part of Stellung Oktavian in Săftica, Romania, used in the defense of the Ploesti oil refineries in 1944.

Early warning of impending bomber raids was provided by these massive Wassermann S (*Cylinder Chimney*) positioned along the coast facing England. This example from Stellung Tausenfüssier of 12./Luft. Nachr.Rgt.53 on the French coast near Théville was upgraded with the Klein Heidelberg antenna to reduce the vulnerability of the radar to Allied Window jamming.

boxes and so make the dispersed bombers more vulnerable to the single-engine fighters. With the growing strength of USAAF escort fighters in early 1944, the German heavy fighters became increasingly ineffective.

In May 1944, the daily operational strength of I.Jagdkorps averaged 450 single engine and 150 heavy fighters; monthly combat losses were 419 aircraft or about 70 percent the force. The attrition rate grew to a staggering 11 percent per mission. The lost fighters could be replaced, the pilots could not. This situation only grew worse and the overall average monthly loss rate for fighters in the West went from 45 percent monthly in 1943 to a gruesome 82 percent in 1944. The Luftwaffe single-engine fighter force suffered catastrophic losses from the last quarter of 1943 at 1,052 fighters, 2,180 in the first quarter of 1944, 3,057 in the second quarter of 1944, and a staggering 4,043 fighters in the third quarter of 1944.

To put this in some perspective, the Luftwaffe lost more single-engine fighters in the West in three months from July to September 1944 than they lost in two whole years on the Russian front from September 1942 to September 1944. Luftwaffe fighter pilot losses were grim, for example 462 crewmen lost in May, including 275 dead and 185 wounded or about three of every five pilots.

The panacea for the day-fighter force was the long-anticipated arrival of jet and rocket fighters. On July 25, 1944, one of the new Me 262 jet fighters saw its combat debut, attacking an RAF Mosquito flying near Munich. On July 28, 1944, seven Me 163 rocket fighters were first observed during a US bombing raid on the Leuna oil complex. The jet and rocket fighters made up only a tiny fraction of the day-fighter force through 1944. Aside from scattered use by training units and the KG (J) 51 fighter-bomber unit, the first Me 262 fighter squadron, JG 7, did not become operational until late November 1944. Their slow arrival was due to technological immaturity and production difficulties. Of the two, the Me 262 was the more promising design, offering excellent speed, range, and firepower. However, its engine design was immature. Both fighters came at a time when the German aircraft industry was under considerable stress. Assembling a high-tech fighter in crude dispersed plants led to severe quality control issues. Further problems were caused when forced labor and slave labor was used to accelerate production. The main operational issue was the short lifespan of the Me 262's Jumo 004 engine, which averaged only 10 to 25 operating hours. The original Jumo 004A had a more acceptable engine life, but the standard Jumo 004B used only about a third of the high-grade steel, leading to drastically inferior durability.

GERMAN FIGHTER PRODUCTION MAY–DECEMBER 1944									
	May	Jun	Jul	Aug	Sep	Oct	Nov	Dec	Total
Bf 109	1,065	1,230	1,348	1,375	1,605	1,583	1,463	1,086	10,755
Fw 190	841	944	1,267	1,391	1,391	1,091	1,291	1,248	9,464
Me 163	1	3	12	13	35	61	22	90	237
Me 262	17	13	16	17	25	28	19	23	158
Me 110	158	110	148	141	188	103	99	58	1,005
Me 410	89	114	102	63	40				408
He 219	17	13	16	17	25	28	19	23	158
Other*	24	22	45	3	66	79	82	102	423
Total	2,212	2,449	2,954	3,020	3,375	2,973	2,995	2,630	22,608

*Other twin-engine fighters such as Ju 88C, Do 335, Ta 154

The Luftwaffe had a difficult time translating its increased 1944 fighter production into new fighter units. The main bottleneck was pilot training. This resulted from endemic fuel shortages which only grew worse with time, especially after the start of the Oil Campaign. To stretch this finite resource, the Luftwaffe chose quantity over quality, continuously cutting back on flight training time. As a result, 1,662 new single-seat fighter pilots were trained in 1942, increasing to 3,276 in 1943. But training fell from about 200 hours in late 1942–early 1943 to about 175 hours in mid 1943–1944. In contrast, Allied training actually increased and averaged 320 hours or more. The discrepancy was greatest in flight-time on operational types, with Luftwaffe pilot hours falling from about 40 to 30 hours while USAAF pilots went from about 75 to 125 hours.

Luftflotte 3 commander Generalfeldmarschall Hugo Sperrle later admitted that the Luftwaffe was more seriously handicapped by a dearth of experienced pilots than a shortage of aircraft. In July of 1944 he canvassed his command and found that, with rare exceptions, only Gruppe and Staffel commanders had combat experience exceeding six months. A small percentage of other personnel had an average of three months of combat duty, while a majority of pilots had seen active service for periods as low as 8–30 days.

Luftwaffe daylight tactics

German fighter tactics against USAAF heavy bombers evolved from 1943 through 1944. In early 1943, the usual tactic was to attack the bombers from the front due to their weak frontal armament. This began to change by mid-1943 with the advent of better forward armament such as the chin-turrets on the B-17 and the nose turret on the B-24. This led to a short period of all-aspect attack before the Luftwaffe developed heavy anti-bomber rockets. The tactics from the summer of 1943 through early 1944 was to attack the bombers from stand-off ranges from the rear. These new rocket weapons were

Searchlights remained in widespread use in 1944–45 as a back-up when fire control radars were jammed. This 150cm Flakscheinwerfer 37 is being operated by Flakwaffen-Helferinnen, women volunteers who served on searchlights, rangefinders, communication systems, and other Flak equipment. Young boys also served as Flak-Helpers, often handling ammunition.

This illustration based on the original handbook drawings shows the new armament package for the Fw 190A-7/R2, A-8/R2, and A-9/R8 assault fighters. A pair of 13mm MG 131 were substituted for the original pair of 7.92mm MG 17 machine guns over the engine (1). The 20mm MG 151 in the wing root (2) remained the same, but a pair of powerful Rheinmetall MK 108 were added in the wing (3). The special Sturmbock versions for new Sturmstaffel close-range attack units added armor plate around the pilot, the engine oil cooler ring, and the 30mm guns as shown here in the blue shaded areas.

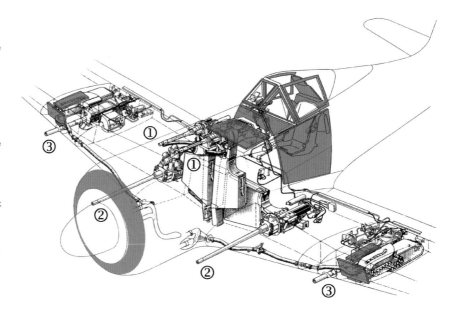

The effectiveness of the Luftwaffe fighters was substantially increased in 1944 due to the increasing use of the powerful Rheinmetall-Borsig MK 108 30mm automatic cannon. The USAAF estimated that it took on average only three hits from one of these guns to shoot down a heavy bomber.

most commonly used on heavy fighters such as the Bf 110, but also on some single-engine fighters. The rockets were extremely potent if detonated near enough to the bomber, but they suffered from significant accuracy issues. Even when the rockets failed to knock down a bomber, their large detonation could serve to break up a bomber formation thereby making the stragglers more vulnerable to single engine fighter swarms. A decisive change in fighter tactics came in early 1944 during Operation *Pointblank* when USAAF escort fighters began to appear over Germany in large numbers. The slow, rocket-armed Luftwaffe fighters were extremely vulnerable to USAAF escort fighters.

The demise of the rocket-armed fighter led the Luftwaffe to focus again on single-engine fighters, especially the new Sturmbock. This was a more heavily armed, armored version of the Fw 190 which would be used to press home attacks at closer range. This led to the formation of Sturmstaffel 1 in June 1943 with plans to add special attack Staffelen in every fighter Geschwader. Tactics shifted to mass attacks, with the individual Gruppe forming a large massed formation called a *Gefechtsverband* (strike formation). Usually, one Staffel of each Gruppe would be instructed to maintain top cover to deal with USAAF escort fighters, while the remainder were assigned to attack the bombers.

In the opinion of many Luftwaffe commanders, this was a serious mistake. Oberstleutnant Hans Kogler, commander of JG 6 in late 1944, later commented: "Orders were given to leave Allied fighters alone and concentrate on the bombers. This command led to a vicious spiral of disaster. The Luftwaffe concentrated on the bombers and were shot down by the fighters. The (US) fighters learned that they were safe against attack and became bolder and more effective. The Luftwaffe headed for the bomber formations that were supposedly not escorted, but you ran into fighters anyway. In the end they were all over the place. The Luftwaffe developed

Besides facing the Luftwaffe over the Balkans, Fifteenth Air Force bombers also were challenged by various German allied air forces including those of Romania, Hungary, and Croatia. This is a Croatian Bf 109 G-14/AS (Werk Nr. 782104) flown by Vladimir Sandtner of 2. Lovačko Jato (fighter squadron), that defected to Falconara, Italy on 16 April 1945.

an inferiority complex which got worse every day but the High Command would not relax the order."

A later US report on the new German tactics concluded that "Enemy units on the whole were too unskilled to accomplish the mass attack. Their formations were haphazard and easily turned. The new tactics did not succeed."

Luftwaffe night tactics

Luftwaffe night-fighter tactics were more dependent on technological factors than the day-fighters. Luftwaffe night-fighters used ground-controlled-intercept (GCI) tactics with a JLO (*Jägerleitoffizier:* fighter control officer) in one of the divisional command posts using the air situation report compiled from the sensor network to direct the night-fighter into the bomber stream. At the start of the Oil Campaign in May 1944, most Luftwaffe night-fighters employed the SN 2 Lichtenstein radar which had an effective range of about 4km.

This process became more complex in the summer of 1943 when the RAF began using Window to jam the Luftwaffe radars. In addition, 100 Group began to employ active jammers such as the Shiver against the Würzburg radar, Mandrel against Freya radars, and Gracer against the SN 2 aircraft radar. The Luftwaffe resorted to early-war tactics, reviving the use of acoustic sound-detectors and searchlights to illuminate the bombers when radars were jammed. With time, the Luftwaffe gradually began to be able distinguish between the faster-moving bombers and the slower Window cloud.

The Ju 88G-6 was the most widely used German night-fighter over Germany in 1944. This provides a good view of the antenna array for the SN-2 Lichtenstein radar on the nose. Here, an American from the USAAF 422nd Night-Fighter Squadron inspects a Ju 88G-6 at Fliegerhorst Langensalza after the fighting.

OPPOSITE DEFENSE OF THE REICH FLAK (JANUARY 1945)

In addition, the Luftwaffe developed its own tricks including the Naxos and Flensburg electronic support measures. The FuG 350 Naxos Z was a passive radar receiver that was able to detect the emissions of the British bomber's H2S navigation radar. This was part of a broader Luftwaffe effort codenamed the Rotterdam Commission, to exploit H2S emissions to help track RAF bomber raids. Besides the aircraft-mounted detectors, ground-based systems were also deployed. The FuG 227 Flensburg radar detector was a passive radar detector that homed in on the signals from the British Monica tail radars added to Bomber Command aircraft in 1943 to detect the approach of German night-fighters. Instead, the Monica became a beacon that attracted the German night-fighters.

The Luftwaffe also experimented with *Wilde Sau* (Wild Boar) tactics that employed single-engine fighters to intercept the bomber stream based on a combination of GCI techniques and visual spotting. Some specialized Wilde Sau tactics were developed in an effort to hunt down the ever-elusive Mosquito bombers used by RAF Bomber Command as the lead wave of the Pathfinder Force.

Luftwaffe Flak

Germany deployed the most lavish Flak forces in the world, including an extensive array of complex heavy artillery and an associated fire control system, first based on searchlights and acoustic sensors, and later on radar. In 1943, Flak constituted 29 percent of the German weapons budget and 20 percent of the munitions budget. The Flak force included half of all Luftwaffe personnel. About 50 to 55 percent of the production of radars and communication equipment, and 33 percent of optical sight production went to Luftwaffe Reich defense.

The Flak force was regionally organized under the Luftgau commands which were regional administrations. By the end of 1943, the Reich defense force included 9 Flak divisions and 4 separate Flak brigades or about 60 percent of the total Flak force. Luftflotte 3 on the approaches to the Reich had a further 3 divisions and 3 separate brigades. The Reich Flak units nearly doubled from 629 heavy Flak batteries in January 1943 to 1,300 in January

The 128mm Flak 40 was the best heavy Flak gun in German service during the war and began to enter service in 1942. This shows a typical G-Stand gun pit of the 14.Flak Division, one of 29 of the division's heavy batteries defending the Leuna synthetic fuel plant.

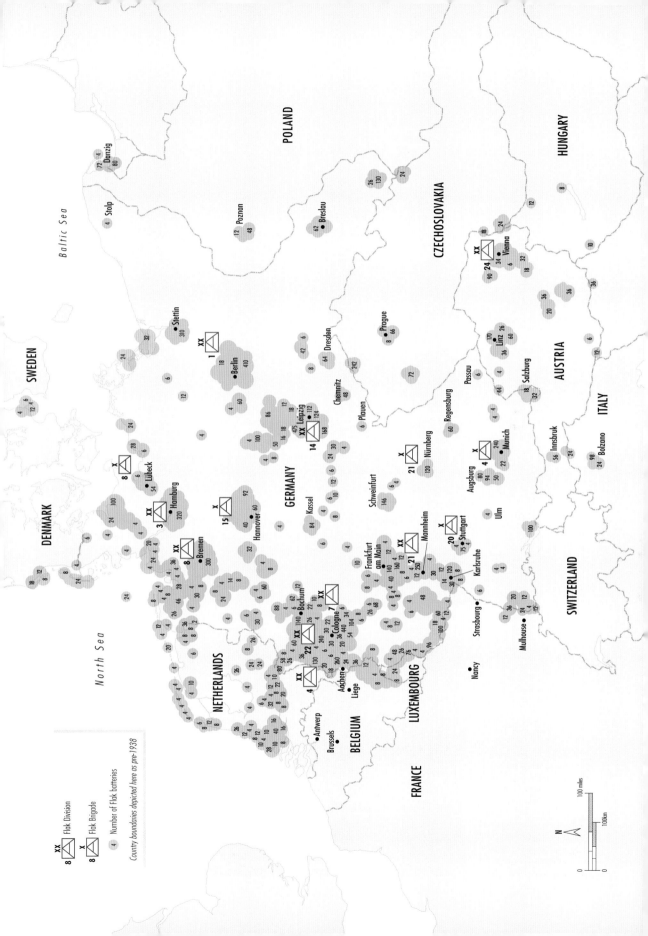

SWEDEN

DENMARK

POLAND

Baltic Sea

North Sea

NETHERLANDS

GERMANY

CZECHOSLOVAKIA

HUNGARY

BELGIUM

LUXEMBOURG

FRANCE

AUSTRIA

SWITZERLAND

ITALY

Danzig
72 4
80

• Stolp 4

Poznan
12
48

Breslau
62
48

26 24
130

8

8

• Stettin 310

XX
▨
1 18 • Berlin
410

24

6
32

12

6

4

60

X
▨
8 6 • Lübeck

XX
▨
3 54 • Hamburg
320

100
24
4
4

Dresden
4 42
6
8 64
242 Prague
8 66

Chemnitz
48

Plauen
6

Leipzig
18 112
47 12 124
16 18 **XX**
50 100 ▨ 168
8 16 **14**
4 30
24
146
Schweinfurt

Linz
170 26
36 60

Salzburg
4
44 18
32

Innsbruck
56 24

Bolzano
98
24

Vienna
88
XX 24 34 62 32
▨ 18
90 **24**

24
36

20 36

8
12

10

12

X
▨
15 40 • Hannover 60
84
4 6
6

Kassel
92
6

32
4

60

4 60

8 12 6

Nürnberg
60 120
Regensburg
Passau
60

X
▨
21 120

Augsburg
80 94
50 22
4 Ulm

Munich
170 240

Mulhouse
24 12

Strasbourg
12 36 20
24 12

Karlsruhe
4 4
75 **20**
X
▨ • Stuttgart
30 120
14 12
30

Mannheim
XX
▨ 12 250
21 160 12
Frankfurt
am Main
4 40 140
8 8
48
8 4 6
60
100 4 12
96 4 8

Nancy

Liege
36 12
• Aachen 24 34
260 54 440
18 4 40 6
XX 130 12
4 8 6
24 24
80 58 26
10 30 4
12 26

XX
▨ Cologne
7 104
20 30 22
40 **XX** 26
22 140 12
88 4

12 Bochum
22 10
62
4 4

6
88
30 4
24 26
4 4 8
36
20
12 6
4 4 10
4 4
26
4 4 16
4 10
28 8
40 16
8
4 4 12
18 12
8

• Antwerp

Brussels •

XX ▨ **8** Flak Division
X ▨ **8** Flak Brigade
● **4** Number of Flak batteries

Country boundaries depicted here as pre-1938

N

100 miles
100km

1944. In spite of their earlier infatuation with Flak, there was growing disquiet amongst senior Nazi leaders over the enormous costs of the Flak force and its meager results during the RAF's devastating summer 1943 Ruhr campaign. The Flak commanders continued to push for upgrades in their armament, especially the trend from the 88mm to 105mm and 128mm gun due to the need to combat USAAF heavy bombers that typically attacked from altitudes of 30,000 feet.

DEFENSE OF THE REICH ORDER OF BATTLE AT START OF OIL CAMPAIGN*		
Luftflotte Reich	Berlin	Generaloberst Hans-Jürgen Stumpff
I.Jagd Korps	Zeist	Generalmajor Josef Schmid
1.Jagddivision	Döberitz	Oberst Günther Lützow
Jagdabschnittsführer-Ostpreussen	Insterburg	Oberstleutnant Karl-Gottfried Nordmann
Jagdabschnittsführer-Schlesien	Cosel	Oberstleutnant Hans-Hugo Witt
2.Jagddivision	Stade	Generalmajor Max-Josef Ibel
Jagdabschnittsführer-Dänemark	Grove	Major Müller-Rendsberg
3.Jagddivision	Deelen (Netherlands)	Generalmajor Walter Grabmann
Jagdabschnittsführer-Mittelrhein	Darmstadt	Oberst Truebenbach
7.Jagddivision**	Schleissheim	Generalmajor Joachim-Friedrich Huth
Jagdabschnittsführer Ostmark	Vienna-Cobenzl	Oberst Hendrix
30.Jagddivision	Berlin	Oberst Hajo Hermann
Luftgaukommando I	Königsberg	General der Flieger Hellmuth Bieneck
Luftgaukommando III	Berlin	General der Flak Gerhard Hoffmann
1.Flak Division	Berlin	Generalleutnant Erich Kressmann
14.Flak Division	Leipzig	Generalleutnant Rudolf Schulze
Luftgaukommando VI	Münster	Generalmajor August Schmidt
4.Flak Division	Duisberg	Generalleutnant Johannes Hintz
7.Flak Division	Cologne	Generalmajor Heinrich Burchard
22.Flak Division	Dortmund	Generalmajor Friedrich Römer
Luftgaukommando VII	Munich	General der Flak Emil Zenetti
4.Flak Brigade	Munich	Generalmajor Ernst Uhl
20.Flak Brigade	Stuttgart	Oberst Wolfgang Bayer
Luftgaukommando VIII	Krakow	General der Flak Walter Sommé
15.Flak Brigade	Posen	Oberst Oskar Krämer
Luftgaukommando XI	Hamburg	General der Flieger Ludwig Wolff
3.Flak Division	Hamburg	Generalmajor Alwin Wolz
8.Flak Division	Bremen	Generalleutnant Kurt Wagner
8.Flak Brigade	Wismar	Oberst Ernst Martin
15.Flak Brigade	Hanover	Oberst Oskar Krämer
Luftgaukommando XII	Wiesbaden	General der Flak Fritz Heilingbrunner
21.Flak Division	Darmstadt	Generalleutnant Kurt Stüdemann
21.Flak Brigade	Nuremburg	Oberst Hans Jürgens
Luftgaukommando XVII	Vienna	General der Flieger Dörstling
24.Flak Division	Vienna	Generalmajor Fritz Grieshammer

*Does not include the fighter and flak units of Luftflotte 3 headquartered in Paris with 4. and 5. Jagddivision

CAMPAIGN OBJECTIVES
The crucial commodity

The Oil Plan

In the late 1930s, Germany imported about 70 percent of its liquid fuel. There were very modest domestic crude oil sources, and most of Germany's domestic liquid fuel supplies came from synthetic fuels derived from coal. In July 1938, Berlin initiated the Karin Hall plan which aimed to increase domestic fuel supplies from the existing level of about 2 million tonnes to about 11 million tonnes annually. The start of the war further imperiled Germany's liquid fuel supply since about 60 percent of the imported fuel came from sources outside Europe that were cut off due to the Royal Navy's maritime blockade. Not surprisingly, Germany took considerable interest in potential European sources, gradually drawing Romania and Hungary into its orbit in order to secure control of the oil fields around Ploesti and Lake Balaton. The Romanian oil fields eventually supplied about a quarter of Germany's liquid fuel requirements. Germany increased its domestic crude oil production and more than doubled its supply of synthetic fuel. It also ruthlessly pillaged fuel supplies from occupied countries. Of the armed services, the Luftwaffe was the most dependent on synthetic fuel supplies since this was the source of most high-octane aviation fuel. Aviation fuel consumption often exceeded production, leading to a gradual drain on reserve stocks.

The Royal Air Force had recognized the vulnerability of Germany's fuel supply since the beginning of the war in 1939. A number of the RAF bombing raids in 1940–41 were directed against the German fuel industry. The collapse of the daylight bombing campaign due to high losses put an end to this campaign. The German plants responsible for fuel production and processing were too small to be attacked at night using the technology of 1942–43.

The USSTAF renewed the Allied focus on German fuel supplies. The most obvious target was the Ploesti oil complex. This was attacked by Operation *Tidal Wave* on August 1, 1943.[3]

Flak batteries were moved periodically depending on the focus of the Allied bombing campaigns. This is a reinforced field position for an 88mm Flak gun of the 7.Flak Division stationed near Neuss and captured in March 1945 during the fighting along the Rhine. The gun is typical of wartime static Flak units, with a simple Sockellafette mount rather than the more complex and expensive mobile cruciform mount.

3   Steven Zaloga, *Ploesti 1943: The Great Raid on Hitler's Romanian Refineries*, (Air Campaign 12), Osprey, 2019.

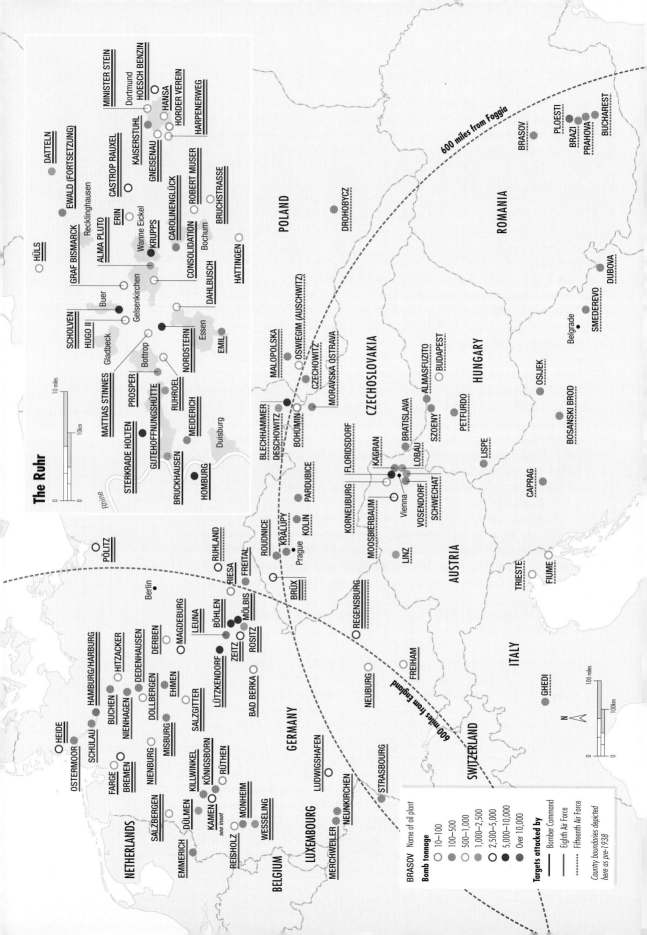

OPPOSITE THE OIL CAMPAIGN BY ALLIED STRATEGIC AIR FORCES APRIL 1944–APRIL 1945

The effects of the *Tidal Wave* mission were disappointing. In spite of significant damage to the refineries, the Romanians had so much redundant capability that it had practically no effect on fuel supplies to Germany. The lesson of the Ploesti raid was that the oil industry would require sustained attack, not a single raid.

The chief advocate of a new campaign against the German fuel industry was Gen. Carl Spaatz, the commander of the USSTAF. Spaatz viewed such a campaign as the logical outgrowth of Operation *Pointblank*. Beyond targeting Luftwaffe aircraft production, a campaign against German fuel supplies would cripple the Luftwaffe's ability to conduct operations. The main reasons for the slow pace of initiating the Oil Campaign were competing requirements.

In March 1944, the USSTAF Special Planning Committee recommended that the heavy bombers be used against the German fuel industry as a means to cripple the mobility of the German army and Luftwaffe in the forthcoming Normandy campaign. The proponents of the "Oil Plan" argued that the destruction of 14 synthetic fuel plants and 13 refineries would cut 80 percent of German production and 60 percent of readily usable refining capacity. Spaatz also wanted to attack the oil targets since he felt that it would coax the Luftwaffe to resist any such campaign, leading to further attrition of the Luftwaffe fighter force. Senior commanders in the RAF argued that the German fuel industry was too dispersed and would take too long to cripple before its effects would be felt on the Normandy battlefield.

The Combined Bomber Offensive and Operation *Pointblank* formally ended on April 1, 1944. This marked a command transition of the strategic bomber forces from control by the Combined Chiefs of Staff to control by Eisenhower's SHAEF (Supreme Headquarters Allied Expeditionary Force). Eisenhower demanded that the strategic bomber forces be put under his direct chain-of-command to support Operation *Overlord*, the invasion of France in the summer of 1944. Eisenhower's deputy, Air Marshal Arthur Tedder, was not convinced of the need to start the Oil Campaign. He maintained that missions in April– May 1944 would be more productive in supporting *Overlord* if aimed at disrupting the railway network between Germany and France to prevent the Wehrmacht from reinforcing its forces near the beachhead. Tedder won Eisenhower's approval for this approach, called the Transportation Plan.

Gardening the Danube

To halt the delivery of Romanian oil to Germany, the RAF's 205 Group conducted "Gardening" missions along the Danube in the summer of 1944, dropping anti-ship mines into the river. These mines, including the 1,000lb Mk. V and 1,850 lb Mk. IV magnetic/acoustic mines, were nicknamed "Cucumbers" by the bomber crews. The first "Gardening" mission was conducted on the night of April 8–9, 1944 by three RAF Liberators and 19 Wellington bombers, delivering 40 mines along the Danube starting near Belgrade. Gardening missions could only be flown on nights with a full moon since the aircraft had to fly no higher than 200 feet to properly deposit the mines. In April, a total of 177 mines were delivered in three missions and in June a further 354 mines were planted in the Danube. These mines were especially effective in the early months of the campaign since the Germans were unprepared to deal with this new threat. In May, a further 225 were dropped during 51 sorties. Exports from the Danube region to Germany and Austria, mainly oil products, fell from 96,000 tonnes in January 1944 to only 21,000 tonnes in May 1944 due to the severe disruption in river traffic. Numerous tankers, tugs, barges, and passenger ships were sunk, and many others were damaged when the RAF bombers conducted low-altitude strafing attacks after their mine delivery. This illustration shows a Gardening mission by a Wellington Mk. X of 205 Group.

The crew of a B-24J piloted by Capt. Howard Slaton of the 755th Squadron, 453rd Bomb Group return to their base in Horsham St. Faith in England after a mission over Germany in the summer of 1944.

A further diversion of the strategic bomber force was the initiation of Operation *Crossbow*.[4] This was the air campaign to smash German missiles sites in France starting in early 1944. Once again, Harris and Spaatz argued that these targets were better suited to the tactical air forces. Nonetheless, the heavy bombers were also diverted away from their strategic objectives to attack these sites.

Spaatz was particularly incensed that the Fifteenth Air Force, based in Italy, was roped into attacks on "political" targets in the Balkans based on British Air Ministry demands. Its bases were too distant from Normandy to have any role in the *Overlord* campaign, but at least on paper, it was committed to supporting the Transportation Plan by attacking various transportation targets in the Balkans. After repeated refusals by Air Chief Marshall Charles Portal of the Air Ministry to permit renewed attacks of Ploesti, Spaatz turned to bureaucratic subterfuge. Once sufficient escort fighters had arrived in Italy, the Fifteenth Air Force started raids against the Ploesti facilities in the guise of attacking neighboring railroads and "transportation" targets. An Army Air Forces Evaluation Board later justified this approach by noting that "The direction of flight…plus the compactness of the target area made bomb spillage in the refinery well nigh inevitable." The new Ploesti offensive began on April 5, 1944 and a total of three raids were conducted in April 1944.

An important but often ignored aspect of the new campaign against Ploesti was the activity of the RAF 205 Group. This group was subordinate to the Fifteenth Air Force and generally conducted missions in Italy. However, in the spring of 1944, the 205 Group began an innovative and highly successful campaign of mining the Danube River to prevent oil and fuel shipments from Ploesti to Germany.

Resistance to the Oil Plan gradually weakened in April. During a British War Cabinet meeting on April 3, Churchill was dismayed to learn that Bomber Command had estimated that the Transportation Plan would cause 80,000 to 160,000 French civilian casualties from attacks on key marshalling yards by the heavy bombers since they tended to be located in urban areas. For the time being, *Crossbow* missions received priority instead. While the role of the heavy bombers in the Transportation Plan was in doubt, Spaatz had a meeting with Eisenhower arguing his case for a start of the Oil Plan. Eisenhower echoed Tedder's objections but Spaatz threatened to resign if senior commanders continued to thwart his efforts to direct the USSTAF. As a compromise, on April 20, Tedder approved a plan that the Eighth Air Force would hit *Crossbow* targets on the next day of clear weather, and then would be free to conduct two missions to hit oil targets in Germany.

4   Steven Zaloga, *Operation Crossbow: Hunting Hitler's V-weapons*, (Air Campaign 5), Osprey, 2018.

THE CAMPAIGN
Collapsing the German war economy

Mission 353: May 12, 1944

The Eighth Air Force had to wait until Friday, May 12 for sufficiently clear weather to conduct the first attack on German synthetic fuel plants. The attack included 886 bombers from all three bomber divisions, hitting 13 separate fuel facilities. Escort would be provided by 735 Eighth and 245 Ninth Air Force fighters.

A post-strike image of the Braunkohle-Benzin AG plant in Bohlen after the May 12, 1944 raid.

By now, escort tactics were being honed to a fine art. Since the fighters flew at higher cruise speeds than the bombers, it was uneconomical to have them fly directly alongside the bombers. Instead, fighter groups were assigned to three phases of the mission. In the initial penetration phase, shorter-ranged fighters escorted the bombers to the German frontier. At this point, the first group of fighters returned to base after being replaced by a larger numbers of fighter groups to conduct escort during the target attack. As the bombers withdrew, the target support fighters were then free to attack targets of opportunity in Germany before returning to base, while a third batch of fighter groups provided escort to the bombers during the withdrawal phase.

On the Luftwaffe side, Generalmajor Josef Schmid, commander of 1.Jagdkorps, finally managed to convince Generaloberst Hans-Jürgen Stumpff, the head of Luftflotte Reich, to centralize all of the divisional fighter direction centers under his I.Jagdkorps. This primarily involved subordinating the 7.Jagddivision in southern Germany that had previously been autonomous. The aim of this was to centralize the deployment of *Gefechstverbanden*, massed fighter forces, to strike the American bombers in unison. In addition, Schmid received permission to use single-engine "Wilde Sau" (wild boar) night-fighters in the day battle. JaFü Ostmark out of Austria added three Gruppen of fighters to the air battles that day.

As a result, the Luftwaffe response on May 12 was the first time that a concentrated effort by the entire Reich force was achieved. A total of 515 fighters took part including 40 twin-engine fighters. In the first wave, 419 fighters reached the bomber stream. Of these, I.Jagdkorps totaled 333 sorties with 266 fighters seeing combat. May 12 was in many ways the swansong of the Reich fighter force. It was the largest single concentration of German Reich defense fighters during the entire air campaign.

A remarkable view as a Me 410B-2/U4 of ZG 26 flies past a B-17G during an air battle over the Brüx synthetic fuel plant on May 12, 1944. This photo was taken from the radio compartment window of the B-17G-BO Flying Fortress named "Lady Godiva" of the 562nd Bomb Squadron, 388th Bomb Group.

Luftwaffe radar stations along the Dutch coast had monitored the formation of the bomber force as they assembled over England. Mission 353 arrived over Dutch coast around 1235. However, Luftflotte Reich abstained from contesting the attack near the coast except for Flak. The plan was to attack the bombers only after they were inside Germany. Around noon, Luftflotte Reich sent instructions to the divisional centers to prepare to dispatch their Gefechtsverbanden, with the heaviest concentration in the vicinity of Frankfurt.

Mission 353 included a diversionary attack on Cologne 1310, but this did not fool the Germans and attracted few German fighters. The Cologne attack was noteworthy in that it was the combat debut of the secret GB-1 guided glide bomb by the 41st Combat Wing. These new guided-weapons were a disappointing flop.[5]

Since 3.Jagddivision was closest to the "bomber Autobahn," they were instructed to form the lead Gefechtsverband. Oberst Walter Oesau, one of the top Luftwaffe aces and commanding officer of JG 1, had been shot down and killed the day before by USAAF escort fighters. As a result, the initial Gefechtsverband was led by Oblt. Rüdiger von Kirchmayr, commander of 5./JG 1. The fighters of JG 1 were reinforced by Gefechtsverband Dachs (Badger) consisting of II./JG 27 and II./JG 53.

The usual practice at this time was to attack the bombers with the better-armed Fw 190 fighters and to use the lighter Bf 109 fighters against the American escort fighters. As a result, III./JG 1 attempted to intercept the escorting P-47 fighters of the 78th Fighter Group while the other two Gruppen headed for the B-24 bombers of the 2nd Bomber Division. The initial contact began around 1320 over the Eifel region near Bonn. The German fighters were hit by the escort fighters before they reached the bombers, and 11 Bf 109 fighters were lost in this melee. Only the II./JG 1 managed a head-on attack. JG 1 claimed 4 B-24s and 1 P-47 shot down, plus 4 B-24 "shot out of formation."

The Luftwaffe had a complicated point scoring system for fighter claims against 4-engine bombers. The most obvious was "shot down" (*Abschüße*). The other two categories were "shot out of formation" (*HSS/Herausschüsse*) and destruction of a damaged straggler (*e.V./endgültige Vernichtungen*).

The heaviest concentration of German fighters occurred in the vicinity of Frankfurt-Wiesbaden-Andernach. The 1.Jagddivision Gefechtsverband was led by Major Friedrich-Karl "Tutti" Müller, commander of JG 3. This formation consisted of three Gruppen of Bf 109 and one of Fw 190 of JG 3. They were reinforced by some single-seat night-fighters of JG 302. In the vicinity was the 2.Jagddivision Gefechtsverband consisting of two Gruppen of Fw 190 and one of Bf 109 from JG 11.

5   Steven Zaloga, *American Guided Missiles of World War II*, Osprey New Vanguard 283: 2020.

The six Gruppen found the 3rd Bomb Division west of Frankfurt and began head-on attacks with five Gruppen starting at 1328. There was a critical gap in USAAF escort coverage of about 15 minutes between the time that the penetrating support escorts headed home and the target support escorts arrived. The absence of escort fighters permitted the German fighters to concentrate on the bombers. The 3rd Bomb Division was the most severely hit, especially the 96th and 452nd Bomb Groups. In the space of less than 15 minutes, JG 3 claimed 24 B-17s shot down and 13 "shot out of formation." The fighters from JG 11 claimed 12 B-17 and two more "shot out of formation". In total, the 3rd Bomb Division lost 41 bombers, by far the heaviest casualties of any of the divisions taking part in Mission 383.

The melee near Frankfurt also included an example of an "ace-on-ace" fighter duel. Maj. Günther Rall had taken over command of II./JG 11 in April 1944. He was an experienced Russian front veteran and would survive the war as the third-highest ace with 275 kills. But he had no experience fighting with the USAAF. That morning, he led the *Stab Schwarm* (headquarters flight) that was on patrol at about 11,000 meters to deal with the American escort fighters. Below him, he spotted the P-47 Thunderbolts of 56th Fighter Group, led by fighter ace Col. Hub Zemke. Rall's flight dove on the Americans, and Rall shot down one of Zemke's wingmen. A neighboring flight of P-47s intervened and chased after Rall from 8,000 meters to tree-top level. His Bf 109 suffered several hits including a round that shattered his hand. He bailed out at 500 meters. After an extensive hospital stay, he returned to flight duty late in 1944. He was lucky; all three other pilots of Stab Schwarm were shot down and killed that day. In total, JG 11 lost 11 Bf 109 fighters including the aircraft of Hptm. Rolf Hermichen, a top ace and commander of I./JG 11.

The 3rd Bomb Division began its attacks around 1400 starting with raids on the synthetic plants in Zwickau and Chemnitz. The deepest target for the 3rd Bomb Division was the Sudetenländische Treibstoffwerke AG at Brüx in the Czech lands. This was hit by 140 bombers dropping 310 tons of bombs.

The 1st Bomb Division bombed the I.G. Farbin AG synthetic fuel plant at Merseburg-Leuna around 1430 totaling 224 bombers. Collateral damage included the top-secret building at Merseburg-Leuna producing heavy water for the German nuclear program. The 92nd and 93rd Combat Wings with 87 bombers hit the Wintershall AG synthetic fuel plant at Lützkendorf. The division lost two bombers.

Starting at 1500, the 14th and 96th Combat Wings of the 2nd Bomb Division totaling 115 bombers attacked the Braunkohle-Benzin AG synthetic fuel plant at Zeitz. A total of 99 bombers hit the neighboring Böhlen plant. During the 2nd Bomb Division attacks raids, 3 B-24s were lost, and 5 damaged beyond repair. Casualties were 7 wounded and 33 missing.

Besides the large-scale Luftwaffe fighter activity, the fuel plants were well defended by Flak. Total Flak activity on May 12 was 399 heavy batteries firing 32,000 rounds and 63 light batteries firing 16,770 rounds.

Overall, the 1.Jagdkorps claimed 36 bombers and 11 fighters shot down by Luftwaffe fighters plus 20 more bombers shot down by Flak. Actual USSTAF casualties for the day were 46 bombers and 14 fighters. The I.Jagdkorps losses were 78 fighters shot down or damaged in the air beyond repair (44+34) and 17 destroyed on the ground. Escorting P-38s claimed 2 German fighters, the P-47s claimed 26, and P-51s claimed 33 in the air and 5 on the ground.

The May 12 raids on the hydrogenation plants had been very effective. The Zeitz plant was hardest hit and lost 16 weeks of output. The Brüx and Tröglitz plants were shut down and lost seven weeks output while the Böhlen and Leuna plants lost half or more of their capacity.

The Luftwaffe clearly understood the significance of Mission 353. The Luftwaffe staff had already warned about the consequences of an attack on the synthetic fuel plants. The only mystery was why the Allies had waited so long. Armament minister Albert Speer later noted that "I shall never forget the day the technological war was decided. Until then, we

Map labels:
- 1
- 2
- 3 2 1
- ENGLISH CHANNEL
- NETHERLAND
- BELGIUM
- Escort fighters
- JG 26
- 4
- 3
- Cologne
- 5
- 6
- JG 27

Luftwaffe Day-Fighter Units	
Jagddivision	Geschwader*
1. Jagddivision	JG 3
2. Jagddivision	JG 11
2. Jagddivision	JG 26
3. Jagddivision	JG 1
3. Jagddivision	JG 26
7. Jagddivision	JG 3
7. Jagddivision	JG 5
7. Jagddivision	JG 53
8. Jagddivision	JG 27

*Some Geschwaderen had dispersed Staffelen in different Jagddivisionen

Key:

- 3rd Bomb Division
- Escort fighters
- 2nd Bomb Division
- 1st Bomb Division

EVENTS

1 Mission 353 began around 1000 as bombers began the assembly process over England. The first groups crossed English coast at 1155 and arrived over the Dutch coast around 1235.

2 One fighter group was assigned to each task force to provide escort during the penetration phase.

3 Force 5 of the 1st Bomb Division conducted a diversionary attack on Cologne around 1310, but attracted few German defenders.

4 German Me 410 heavy fighters of JG 26 attempted an early interception, but were kept away from the bombers by the escort fighters.

5 The escort fighters providing penetration support departed with the arrival of a larger force of 11 fighter groups to provide target support.

6 The initial German fighter attacks by JG 1 began around 1320 over the Eifel region west of Frankfurt. The German fighters were hit by the escort fighters before they reached the 2nd Bomb Division, and 11 Bf 109 fighters were lost in this melee, claiming to have shot down four B-24s and 1 P-47.

7 The heaviest concentration of German fighters occurred in the vicinity of Frankfurt-Wiesbaden-Andernach including about six fighter Gruppen in two Gefechtsverbanden of the 1. Jagddivision and 2.Jagddivision. The German fighters began attacks on the 3rd Bomb Division starting at 1328. There was a critical gap of about 15 minutes in USAAF escort coverage between the time support escorts headed home and target support escorts arrived. This permitted unrestrained attacks on Force 2, leading to the loss of more than two dozen bombers.

8 After enduring the heaviest losses of the mission, the 3rd Bomb Division began its bomb runs around 1400 hitting the synthetic fuel plant in Chemnitz and Zwickau. The deepest target for the mission was the Sudetenländische Treibstoffwerke AG at Brüx in the Czech lands, hit by 140 bombers.

9 The 1st Bomb Division bombed the I.G. Farbin AG synthetic fuel plant at Merseburg-Leuna around 1430 totaling 224 bombers while 87 bombers struck the Wintershall AG synthetic fuel plant in nearby Lützkendorf.

10 Starting at 1500, a total of 116 bombers of the 2nd Bomb Division bombed the Braunkohle-Benzin AG synthetic fuel plant at Zeitz while 99 bombers hit the neighboring Böhlen plant.

11 Flak defenses over the targets claimed 20 bombers during Mission 353.

12 On exiting the strike area, the escort fighters of the Target Support groups dispersed to attack targets of opportunity on their way back to England while the Withdrawal Support groups arrived to continue escorting the bombers on their return flight to England.

The Oil Campaign begins: Mission 353, May 12, 1944

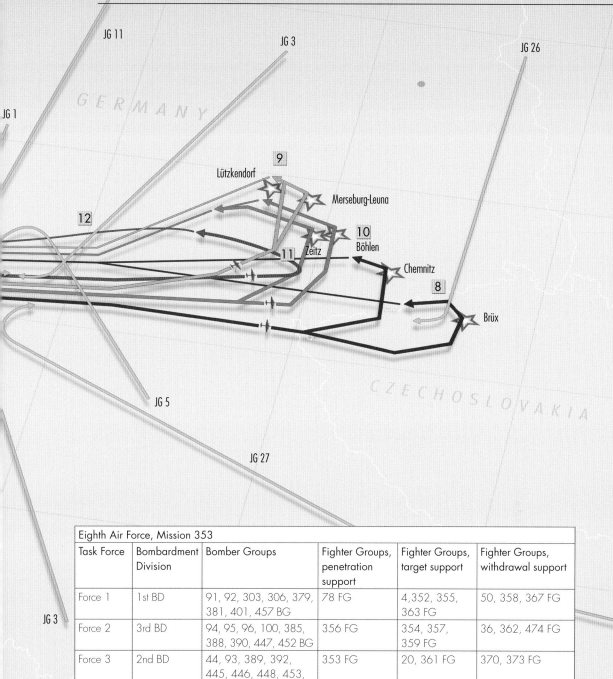

Eighth Air Force, Mission 353					
Task Force	Bombardment Division	Bomber Groups	Fighter Groups, penetration support	Fighter Groups, target support	Fighter Groups, withdrawal support
Force 1	1st BD	91, 92, 303, 306, 379, 381, 401, 457 BG	78 FG	4, 352, 355, 363 FG	50, 358, 367 FG
Force 2	3rd BD	94, 95, 96, 100, 385, 388, 390, 447, 452 BG	356 FG	354, 357, 359 FG	36, 362, 474 FG
Force 3	2nd BD	44, 93, 389, 392, 445, 446, 448, 453, 458, 466, 467, 492, 492 BG	353 FG	20, 361 FG	370, 373 FG
Force 4	3rd BD	34, 487, 486 BG	479 FG	55, 339 FG	19, 65, 129, 306 FG, 315 Sqd RAF
Force 5	1st BD	303, 379, 384 BG	364 FG	406 FG	406 FG

(Note on altitudes: Missions were conducted at an altitude around 30,000 feet)

had managed to produce as many weapons as the Wehrmacht needed, in spite of their considerable losses. But with the attack of the 935 daylight bombers of the American Eighth Air Force upon several fuel plants in central and eastern Germany, a new era in the air war began. It meant the end of German armaments production." On May 19, Speer reported to Hitler that "The enemy has struck us at one of our weakest points. If they persist at it this time, then we will soon no longer have any fuel production worth mentioning. Our one hope is that the other side has an air force general staff as scatterbrained as ours."

The effects of the May 12 raid were immediate. The Luftwaffe operations staff in Berlin began transferring light and heavy Flak guns from the Russian front to reinforce the synthetic fuel plants at Zeitz and Pölitz. As importantly, this message was intercepted by the Allies and decrypted by the Ultra codebreaking teams at Bletchley Park. This message confirmed Spaatz's assertions about the value of the synthetic fuel plants to the German war effort. A week later, another message was intercepted informing the Wehrmacht that support vehicles would have to be converted to use inefficient wood fuel generators due to shortages of liquid fuel. On reading these decrypts, Air Marshal Tedder finally relented from his opposition to Spaatz's Oil Plan and acknowledged that "I guess we will have to give the customer what he wants."

The bombing attacks not only affected the Luftwaffe, but the Kriegsmarine as well. On May 21, the Marine-Gruppenkommando West, responsible for naval operations in the North Sea and Channel coast, were warned to expect cut-backs in fuel and lubricants in June due to the attacks on Ploesti and the German synthetic fuel plants. The headquarters of Admiral Black Sea was warned that no fuel would be provided in June. Both these messages were intercepted and decrypted by the Ultra code-breakers.

On May 15, Luftwaffe chief Hermann Göring met with Beppo Schmid of I.Jagdkorps and fighter inspector Adolf Galland to discuss possible improvements in the face of the new American campaign against the synthetic fuel plants. Galland suggested transferring two Jagdgruppen from the Russian front to Reich defense, but Göring would only agree to the transfer of II./JG 5 and IV./JG 54, less than a third of the request. This reinforcement was pitifully small and was reflective of the desperate state of the Luftwaffe fighter force in the wake of Operation *Pointblank*.

The Luftwaffe had intended to bolster Gruppe strength from the existing level of 40 to 68 fighters. But at this stage of the war, the average strength was only 31 and declining, so the new objective was never reached. Göring also agreed to Galland's proposal to dissolve the two Wilde Sau single-seat night-fighter Gruppen and disperse the pilots and personnel to the other fighter groups. Göring did not agree with Galland's proposal to transfer Luftflotte three fighter units to Reich Defense since this would strip the Invasion Front of fighter cover prior to the anticipated Allied summer amphibious landings. Galland pointed out that the supply of new pilots for Reich defense was less than the combat losses. The Reich defense units were typically losing 10 percent more of its fighters per daylight mission against the Eight Air Force. In contrast, American bomber losses were about 2 percent per mission. Galland wanted all fit pilots serving on staff positions to be returned to flight duty, transfer 80–100 instructors to flight duty, and transfer some night-fighter pilots to day-fighters. To make matters worse, Göring informed the training directorate that their monthly supply of 60,000 tonnes of fuel was being cut back to 50,000 tonnes. The declining fuel supply and transfer of experienced instructors implied that the number of new pilots would decline or the level of training would be cut back, either way diminishing the combat effectiveness of the fighter force.

Schmid's proposals mainly involved further centralization of Reich air defense under his I.Jagdkorps. Control of Flak units was transferred from the Luftgaue to the regional Jagddivision headquarters. Jafü Ostmark in Austria was subordinated to I.Jagdkorps as 8.Jagddivision. The 7.Jagddivision was consolidated by moving its scattered groups from Frankfurt and Munich to a more central location around Ansbach-Bernberg to facilitate the concentrated formation of its Gefechtsverband.

Ploesti attacks resume

In the face of growing evidence of the effectiveness of the Oil Campaign as well as pressure from senior USAAF leaders, RAF leaders including Tedder and Portal began to back away from restrictions on attacks on the Ploesti oil refineries. While the April and early May missions against Ploesti had been conducted under the guise of attacks on transportation targets, the attacks in late May were more honestly reported as strikes against the oil industry.

The May 18 mission was disrupted by poor weather and the planned attack by 700 bombers was reduced to only 206 B-17s and B-24s. On top of the weather, the smoke dischargers at Ploesti proved to be very effective in obscuring the targets. The results of this attack were poor with only eight bombs landing within the Română Americana refinery. The May 26 raid was a night mission by 74 RAF bombers. The most successful mission in May took place on May 31 when the Fifteenth Air Force hit four refineries with 481 bombers. The Concordia Vega refinery was struck by 156 bombs, destroying the boiler house and putting the plant out of operation for more than two weeks. Română Americana was hit by 37 bombs, damaging the boiler house and crippling operations for a month.

Spaatz wanted to stage the second Oil Campaign mission on May 13 but the weather over central and eastern Germany did not turn favorable for another two weeks. Mission 376 took place on Sunday, May 28, 1944 and included 1,341 bombers and 1,224 escort fighters. As in the case of the first oil mission, the second mission included a diversionary raid against Cologne by the 1st Bomb Division. The other missions largely duplicated the May 12 mission, aimed at a wide variety of synthetic fuel plants in central and eastern Germany.

B-24J bombers of the Fifteenth Air Force attack the Concordia Vega refinery in Ploesti during Mission A67 of May 31, 1944. This mission included 53 B-17 and 42 B-24 bombers dropping 1,115.6 tons of bombs. A total of 16 bombers were lost on this mission, with 13 lost to Flak. The white smoke plumes in the center were from Romanian smoke pots intended to obscure the refinery from aerial attack.

Due to the steady attrition from air battles earlier during the month, the Luftwaffe could only put up 333 fighters on May 28 compared to 515 on March 12. The I.Jagdkorps vectored its forces into a great mass near Magdeburg. Oberstleutnant Rüdiger von Kirchmayr, commander of 5./JG 1, formed up the lead 3.Jagddivision Gefechtsverband. Three more Gefechtsverbanden from 1., 2. and 7.Jagddivision joined it, forming an angry swarm of nine Gruppen with about 180 Fw 190 and Bf 109 fighters to attack the bombers. Three more Bf 109 Gruppen formed the high group to deal with the escorts. The Gefechtsverbanden were instructed not to attack the lead American bomber formations but to attack the succeeding formations.

The German formations initially hit the 390th Bomb Group, shooting down six bombers, and seriously damaging several more. P-51 Mustangs of the 357th Fighter Group joined the melee, and were subsequently joined by more fighters from the 4th Fighter Group that had been escorting the lead 1st Bomb Division. In the ensuing dogfights, the USAAF fighters claimed 37 German fighters and 29 probables for a loss of two fighters. Actual German losses from these formations were 37 fighters as well as 13 pilots KIA and 13 WIA. These German totals include fighters that were shot down while returning to base by roaming US fighters.

The heaviest American losses that day were suffered by the 94th Bomb Wing that had departed the main bomber stream to attack targets in the Dessau area. A Gefechtsverband of three Bf 109 Gruppen from Jafü Ostmark arrived after the main 1.Jagdkorps concentration had begun its massed attack. Lacking escort fighters, the B-17s of the 94th Bomb Wing were systematically pummeled by the German fighters, eventually losing 12 bombers. German losses were 7 Bf 109 with casualties of 4 KIA and 2 WIA.

The 205 Group RAF flew with the US Fifteenth Air Force out of bases in Italy and took part in the Oil Campaign in the Balkans including the "Gardening" mine-laying operations. This remarkable shot shows Liberator KK320 of No. 37 Squadron moments before it was accidentally hit by bombs from an aircraft overhead during a raid on Montfalcone. The bombs did not detonate, and the pilot, Squadron Leader L. Saxby, managed to get the heavily damaged bomber back to its base.

The day's attack was costly on both sides with the Eighth Air Force losing 32 bombers and 9 fighters to Luftwaffe fighters and flak. German losses were 52 fighters shot down; overall losses were 78 fighters when adding in those damaged beyond repair. To put this in perspective, a quarter of the German fighter force engaged in missions that day were lost, ten times the loss rate of the US bomber force.

The severe losses suffered by I.Jagdkorps in May 1944 forced the Luftwaffe to comb other fronts for fighter reinforcements in late May 1944. A total of 11 Jagdgruppen from the Russian and Italian fronts were ordered to transfer one Jagdstaffel for Reich defense, a third of their combat strength.

The effect of the May 28 bombing on the oil plants was not as dramatic as on May 12 with only the Zeitz plant being severely damaged. Nevertheless, the May 28 battle showed the diminishing ability of the Luftwaffe to deal with bomber attacks.

The Eighth Air Force returned the next day with Mission 379, a deep attack against the Pölitz plant near Stettin on the Baltic coast as well as a variety of other targets deep into Prussia and western Poland. The bomber stream included 993 bombers and

1,265 escort fighters. Due to the depth of the attack, the 2nd Bombardment Division split off to hit Pölitz while the other divisions hit aviation plants in central Germany. At the same time, the Fifteenth Air Force struck targets in southern Germany and Austria. I.Jagdkorps put up 275 fighters of which 208 fighters took part in the air battles. A total of 101 fighters from the 7.Jagddivision, Jafü Ostpreussen (East Prussia), and Jafü Schlesien (Silesia) headed against the Fifteenth Air Force bomber stream.

The northern air battles led to the loss of 37 USAAF bombers as well as ten fighters. The heaviest losses were suffered by the 2nd Bomb Division that was hit over the Baltic by the Gefechtsverband of 1.Jagddivision, losing 17 bombers. The fighter losses of 1.Jagdkorps were 57 shot down or damaged beyond repair. Among the casualties was JG 3 commander Oberstleutnant "Tutti" Müller whose aircraft stalled and crashed over the airfield; his distraught men blamed his death on his physical and mental exhaustion after a month of nearly continuous combat missions. In the southern battles, the 7.Jagddivision claimed seven bombers for a loss of 24 fighters shot down or damaged beyond repair. The northern attacks were notably successful; the Pölitz plant was put out of operation for two months. Further oil missions were deferred in late May and early June in order to support Operation *Overlord*.

Impact of the initial Oil Campaign

By late May, there was a growing consensus amongst Allied leaders that the Oil Campaign could have a decisive effect on the German war effort. A report by the Joint Intelligence Committee on May 27 concluded that "a concerted and successful attack on German sources of oil production would, within a period from 3–6 months, produce a shortage of oil so serious that it would render it impossible for (Germany) to carry out full operations on three major fronts…Both on the short-term and on the long-term, oil has therefore become a vital factor in German resistance." The British Air Staff responded to this assessment on June 3 by recommending that Bomber Command attack oil plants in the Ruhr as soon as its commitments to Operation *Overlord* permitted.

Ultra decrypts on June 7, one day after the Normandy landings, disclosed that Berlin had warned Luftwaffe units in France that fuel would be restricted to only the most vital units. The fuel situation had become so dire that the Wehrmacht strategic reserve was finally being tapped. The July fuel allotments were in doubt and units were warned that they should expect to depend on available stocks. This Ultra decrypt was judged by the Chief of the Air Staff to be "one of the most important pieces of information we have yet received" and they urged Churchill not to wait but to reassign the combined strategic bomber force against the German oil industry as quickly as possible to precipitate its collapse. Allied intelligence estimated that the normal German synthetic fuel capacity had been reduced from 1,200,000 tons per month to 670,000 tons and that the Wehrmacht required at least 1,000,000 tons per month for operational efficiency. Allied intelligence had recognized that it had finally found a vital target that was exceptionally vulnerable to bomber attack.

German countermeasures

Due to the American air raids, the production of aviation fuel fell from 5,800 tonnes in March 1944 to 623 tonnes per day in June 1944. Under such dire circumstances, Hitler turned to armaments minister Albert Speer to redeem the situation. Speer proposed the creation of small, dispersed plants rather than relying on large and easily targeted conglomerates. Oil industry officials had been recommending the creation of underground facilities since 1940, but due to the expense, this had not been undertaken. Underground facilities were expected to cost three times as much as conventional plants.

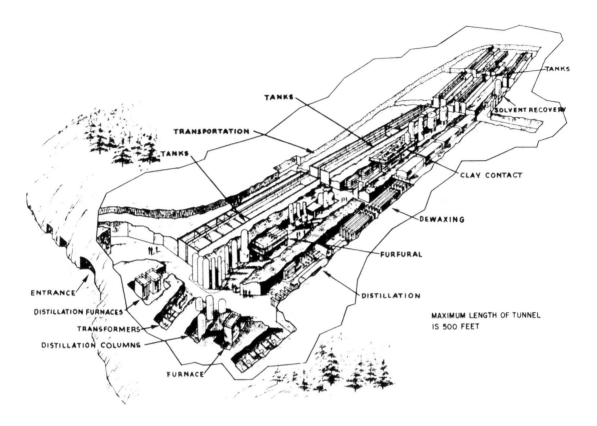

TANKS

TRANSPORTATION

TANKS

TANKS

SOLVENT RECOVERY

CLAY CONTACT

DEWAXING

FURFURAL

DISTILLATION

ENTRANCE

DISTILLATION FURNACES

TRANSFORMERS

DISTILLATION COLUMNS

FURNACE

MAXIMUM LENGTH OF TUNNEL IS 500 FEET

One of the few underground synthetic fuel plants near to reaching completion was the Dachs 1 lubrication oil plant near Porta. Due to the nature of the lubrication oil production process, the entire plant had to be constructed as a unified system in a series of reinforced tunnels as seen in this post-war US intelligence report.

To centralize the efforts to restore the German liquid fuel industry, on May 31, 1944, Speer appointed Edmund Geilenberg, the director of Braunschweig steel-works, as *Generalkommissar für Sofortmaßnahmen* (General Commissioner for Immediate Actions). Geilenberg was given extensive powers, and eventually was authorized by Hitler to apply the death penalty to anyone obstructing his program. Geilenberg took over the administrative staff of BRABAG (Braunkohle Benzin AG) in Berlin, to form the core of the new *Mineralöl-Baugesellschaft mbH* (Synthetic Fuel Construction Company), headquartered in Luckenwalde. Geilenberg's team released a comprehensive plan on August 1, 1944 called the *Mineralölsicherungsplan* (Synthetic Fuel Security Plan) but more popularly known as the Geilenberg Programm.

Geilenberg's special programs eventually included 350,000 workers including a substantial slave labor force. The program consisted of three major projects. The first was a program to rebuild the most important synthetic fuel plants as quickly as possible after each Allied bombing raid. Next, the dispersal program planned to erect forty pairs of small distillation units at twenty scattered locations in mines, caves, or woods. In addition, five distillation plants, each with a capacity of 12,000 tonnes a month, were to be built in five bomb-damaged factories. These were intended to produce motor gasoline and diesel oil for the army and navy, with a goal of 14,000 tonnes of gasoline and 40,000 tonnes of diesel oil a month. The third project aimed at building five massive underground hydrogenation plants, fed on brown coal tar. These in association with several catalytic plants were expected to produce 40,000 tonnes of high-octane aviation fuel per month, including specialized jet fuel. A number of small underground plants were to be created for the production of lubricants. One of its most ambitious efforts was *Unternehmen Wüste* (Operation *Desert*), aimed at creating ten shale oil extraction plants in Württemberg and Hohenzollern.

The Geilenberg Programm eventually proved to be a disappointing flop. The creation of small dispersed plants and new underground plants proved nearly impossible due to the disintegration of German industry under the relentless Allied bombing attacks. The program was paralyzed due to its reliance on railroad transportation to create and supply the plants as well as to move any resulting fuel products. As the German railroad network ground to a halt, so did the construction programs. Feed sources for the plants were lacking and the existing power network could not provide adequate electrical power to operate the new plants.

As a result, the German liquid fuel industry was obliged to make do with existing facilities. A program had already been underway to make the plants more resistant to air attack. The Flak force began a major reshuffle to reinforce the defenses around key fuel plants. In terms of passive defense, blast walls were erected around key assemblies within each plant to limit the damage from nearby hits. As part of the Geilenberg program, large numbers of workers from other industries were dragooned into doing repair work at bombed facilities. This enabled a number of plants to re-establish production in the late summer and early autumn. However, much of this reconstruction was made possible from cannibalizing equipment. As sources of equipment were destroyed during later air raids, reconstruction efforts became impossible by late autumn.

Bomber Command joins the battle

With Allied land forces safely ensconced on the Normandy coast, the priorities for the Allied heavy bomber forces shifted. On June 8, Spaatz made the German fuel industry the first priority for the USSTAF. The flow of Ultra decrypts confirmed the effectiveness of the Oil Campaign and eroded any remaining resistance to the plan from RAF senior commanders, except for Harris. He continued to deride the fuel industry as a "panacea" target, but was obliged to make at least a token effort due to pressure from Churchill and other senior RAF commanders.

RAF Bomber Command began its participation in the Oil Campaign on the night of June 12–13, aimed mainly at plants in the Ruhr industrial region. The first target was the

Four Lancaster bombers of 460 Squadron RAAF, 1 Group at RAF Binbrook prior to a July 1944 mission with AR-P in the foreground. The large cylindrical bomb is a 4000 H.C. (High Capacity) called a "cookie" or "block-buster" and weighing 4,000 pounds. (AWM)

Gelsenberg AG synthetic fuel plant located in Gelsenkirchen. A total of 303 aircraft were assigned to the raid including 271 Lancasters of the 1 and 3 Groups plus a Pathfinder Force of 6 Lancasters of 17 Mosquitoes from 8 Group. The attack benefited from the arrival of an improved version of the Oboe navigation aid that was used by the Mosquitoes of the Pathfinder Force. The marking of the target was exceptionally accurate.

Gelsenkirchen was within the defense sector of the 3. Jagddivision and the forward search radars along the Dutch coast picked up the approaching Bomber Command formation shortly before midnight on June 12/13. The 3.Jagddivision command center alerted NJG 1 which played the principal role in intercepting the British attack. NJG 1 was the first German night-fighter unit to receive the new He 219 Uhu night-fighter, deployed at the time in I./NJG 1 and IV./NJG 1. Hptm. Heinz-Wolfgang Schnaufer of the Stab of IV./NJG 1 flying a Bf 110G intercepted a group of Lancasters near Cambrai and shot down three at low altitude from 1,000 to 1,500 meters in a seven minute engagement starting around 0027. Two He 219 fighters of I./NJG 1 piloted by Hptm. Ernst-Wilhelm Modrow and Leutnant Hittler intercepted departing Lancasters and each shot one down. In total, NJG 1 claimed the destruction of 11 Lancasters that night. The Bomber Command formations involved in the Gelsenkirchen raid lost a total of 17 Lancasters. Some of those not claimed by NGJ 1 may have been lost to Flak, but other German night-fighter units were active that night due to substantial RAF raids to the south around Amiens. NJG 3 claimed two Lancasters in the Duisberg area and NJG 6 claimed two near Deelen that were probably part of the Gelsenkirchen raid. Total Bomber Command losses that night were 17 Halifaxes and 23 Lancasters with German night-fighters claiming to have shot down 41.

The Gelsenkirchen raid was exceptionally destructive and accurate. A total of about 1,500 bombs fell in the factory area, destroying 200,000 tons of synthetic fuel stored at the plant. In addition, the plant was inoperative for several weeks depriving the German war effort of a further thousand tons of aviation fuel each day it was shut down. Repair work gradually brought the plant on line, only to have the Allies bomb it again and again. In fact, subsequent attacks kept it inoperative until it was finally overrun in 1945.

The second Bomber Command raid of the Oil Campaign was not as successful as the first raid. The target on the night of June 16/17 was Ruhrchemie A.G. at Sterkrade-Holten. The mission included 162 Halifaxes of 4 and 6 Groups, 137 Lancasters of 1 and 6 Groups plus a Pathfinder Force of 6 Lancasters and 16 Mosquitoes of the 8 Group. The weather was worse than predicted with cloud cover up to 14,000 feet. When the Pathfinders dropped their Target Indicators, they were enveloped in the cloud base, becoming little more than faint glows.

Unfortunately for Bomber Command, the 3.Jagddivision command post had vectored its force of night-fighters from NJG 1 over a beacon near Bocholt that was only 20 miles to the northwest of the target and along the flight path. The German night-fighters began to converge en masse on the bomber force. The first attacks began at 0053, and continued for the next hour. Luftwaffe night-fighters claimed 36 kills including 24 by NJG 1, 8 by NJG 2 and 3 by NJG 3. Actual losses were 32 bombers, a tenth of the overall force. This included 22 Halifax and 10 Lancasters; the RAF thought about 10 of these were due to Flak. The worst hit was 77 Squadron that lost 7 of its 23 Halifaxes. Hauptman Adolf Breves of the Stab IV./NJG 1 flying a Bf 110G-4 claimed three kills that night and five other pilots claimed double kills. It was a particularly successful night for the new He 219 fighters, accounting for eight of the kill claims. The RAF losses were all the more tragic since the bombing had been largely ineffective with few bombs actually hitting within the plant area.

The third RAF raid of the Oil Campaign was a pair of strikes involving 361 sorties against two separate targets on the night of June 21/22. The attack against the Wesseling synthetic fuel plant came mainly from 5 Group including 128 Lancasters and 6 Mosquitoes plus 5 more Lancasters from 1 Group. The Wesseling plant was marked by 5 Group Mosquitoes

dropping red flares. After the problems over Sterkade-Holten, the bombers were instructed that if the flares were not visible, they were to employ blind bombing tactics using the H2S radars. The Wesseling attack proved to be a frustrating mission due to cloud cover and strong German night-fighter attacks. Of the 133 Lancasters of the Wesseling force, 37 were shot down. German reports indicate that the raid reduced the plant capacity by about 40 percent.

The Scholven/Buer synthetic fuel plant was attacked by 120 Lancasters and 6 Mosquitoes of 5 Group, plus 7 Lancasters of 1 Group, and 5 Pathfinder Mosquitoes of 8 Group. The Scholven raid was less costly than the Weseling attack, with 8 Lancasters lost. However, the target damage was less with capacity reduced by only 20 percent.

Once again, the night-fighters of NJG 1 were in the thick of the fighting, claiming to have shot down 34 Lancasters. This Geschwader first hit the inbound bomber stream over Venlo in the Netherlands around 0112 and continued its interceptions for over an hour including some interceptions over Scholven. Two of its ace pilots, Hptm. Ernst-Wilhelm Modrow and Hptm. Heinz Schnaufer both claimed four kills that night. Three other pilots of the unit claimed triple kills. NJG 3 claimed a total of 14 kills, many of them over the Netherlands before the bombers reached their targets. NJG 2 claimed five bomber kills and overall Luftwaffe kill claims that night were 55 compared with the actual RAF losses of 46 Lancasters. The RAF thought that about ten of their losses were due to Flak, but the actual source of losses was almost impossible to determine under night conditions.

By the end of June, Bomber Command was in serious doubt about their role in the Oil Campaign. Of the four raids, only one seemed to have been effective. Furthermore, the attacks had been prohibitively costly in aircrew and bombers. What was not immediately apparent at the time was that the "Wizard War," the electronic warfare contest, had been tilting in favor of the German night-fighters. The RAF was aware of the combat debut of the new SN 2 Lichtenstein radar after a BF 110G-4 landed in Switzerland in late April 1944. This radar was not as susceptible to Window jamming as previous types.

A Lancaster of No. 467 Squadron RAAF, 5 Group returning to RAF Waddington on August 14, 1944. (AWM)

A far greater prize arrived on the night of July 13, 1944 when a Ju 88G-1 night-fighter of 7./NJG 2 inadvertently took a reciprocal course at the end of a mission, mistakenly landing at an RAF base in Suffolk. Not only did the aircraft give the RAF their first detailed look at the SN 2 radar, but the fighter was also fitted with two electronic support measures, the Naxos and Flensburg. Once the role of the Flensburg was recognized, the Monica radars were removed from RAF bombers.

The RAF responded to the German electronic warfare innovations with new systems of their own, some of which were already in the pipeline. The 100 Group began to employ the Mandrel radar jammer to make it more difficult for Luftwaffe radars to track the bomber formations. New types of Window were introduced to confuse the new German night-fighter radars. Security measures were adopted to reduce the ability of the Luftwaffe to exploit RAF electronic devices, for example instructing crews to avoid use of the H2S radar until well into German territory and to avoid the use of IFF (identification-friend-or-foe) systems.

While Bomber Command pondered new tactics to deal with the deadly night-fighter threat, a number of small raids were conducted by Mosquitoes. On the night of June 25/26, 42 Mosquitoes of 8 Group attacked the Rheinpreussen synthetic fuel plant at Homberg-Meerbeck. No aircraft were lost, but little damage was inflicted. This target was attacked again on the night of July 16/17, once again without loss but with little damage to the target.

Bomber Command returned to the Oil Campaign in force on the night of July 18/19, revisiting the familiar targets of Wesseling and Scholven/Buer. Both of these attacks were effective and bomber losses were relatively light. Bomber Command was not so fortunate two nights later when they attacked two synthetic fuel plants at Homberg and Bottrop. Bottrop, like most of the previous raids, was located in the Ruhr industrial region. However, Homberg presented a more difficult target, located further south in the Saar industrial region. These raids were hit by a concentrated Luftwaffe night-fighter force. Their primary opponents were NJG 1 with 14 claimed kills that night and NJG 3 with 11 bomber claims. The five night-fighter units engaged on July 20/21 claimed 37 bombers; 38 were actually lost including

Bomber Command's principal night-time adversary in the summer of 1944 was the Messerschmitt Bf 110G-4 with the new FuG 220 Lichtenstein SN-2 radar. This is a Bf 110G-4/R3/B2/M2 of 9.NJG 1 with the codes G9+HT (Werk-Nr. 160128) at Fritzlar air base at the end of the war.

nine Lancasters raiding the Courtrai railway yards in France. The hardest hit unit was the 75 (New Zealand) Squadron that lost seven of its 25 Lancasters during the Homberg raid. In spite of the casualties, the Homberg and Bottrop raids were judged to be very effective with accurate and concentrated bombing of the fuel plants. A final raid of the month on July 25/26 was conducted against the Wanne-Eickel plant, without loss.

While Bomber Command debated whether to continue the Oil Campaign in the face of the heavy losses, the first mission of the new month was flown on the night of August 5/6 against the familiar Wanne-Eickel synthetic fuel plant. This mission was conducted by 35 Mosquitoes and appeared to have started a number of fires.

In preparation for further deep raids into Germany, on August 15, Bomber Command staged a massive raid including 599 Lancasters, 385 Halifaxes and 19 Mosquitoes against 9 airfields of the German night-fighter force. The first major Oil Campaign target in August was Sterkade which was attacked on the night of August 18/19 by 4 Group with 210 Halifaxes, 10 Lancasters, and 14 Mosquitoes. Losses were modest compared to the July raids, 1 Halifax, and 1 Lancaster, both claimed by NJG 1. The next raid on August 27 was a complete change from the previous attacks. In light of the heavy night losses in July and the declining Luftwaffe fighter force, Bomber Command decided to attempt its first major daylight raid into Germany since 1941. The target was the Rheinpreussen synthetic fuel plant in Meerback/Homberg. The force consisted of 216 Halifaxes of 4 Group and 14 Mosquitoes and 13 Lancasters of the 8 Group performing the Pathfinder mission. The 2 TAF provided nine squadrons of Spitfires for escort to the target, but only a single Bf 110 was seen and it was driven off. Flak was heavy but ineffective. As often was the case, cloud cover proved to be a problem, but a combination of Oboe navigation and gaps in the cloud permitted some precision bombing.

OIL CAMPAIGN HEAVY BOMBER MISSIONS BY BOMBER COMMAND IN JULY–AUGUST 1944			
Date	Target	Sorties*	Bomber losses
Jul			
18/19	Wesseling	194+6	1
18/19	Scholven	170+13	4
20/21	Homberg	158+11	20
20/21	Bottrop	166+13	8
25/26	Wanne-Eickel	135+10	0
Aug			
5/6	Wanne-Eickel	0+35	0
18/19	Sterkade	220+14	2
27	Homberg	229+14	0
Total		1,307+81	35

*Heavy bombers + Mosquitoes

Post-invasion USSTAF Oil Campaign

The Eighth Air Force was heavily committed to the support of Operation *Overlord* during the last days of May and first two weeks of June 1944. The first major Oil Campaign operation following the invasion was Mission 421 on June 18, 1944. The principal targets were oil refineries in Hamburg and Misburg for the 1st and 3rd Bomb Division while the 2nd Bomb Division was assigned refineries in Bremen, the Luftwaffe control center at the Faßberg air base, and 2.Jagddivision's Sokrates control center in Stade. The mission included

1,378 bombers and 817 escort fighters. The weather deteriorated during the approach to the target areas and many of the attacks were based on blind bombing led by the Pathfinders. A total of 11 bombers and three fighters were lost, almost all due to Flak thanks to a lack of any fighter activity by 1.Jagdkorps owing to the weather.

The situation was significantly different two days later on Mission 425. This was another large, dispersed attack against a variety of oil and industrial targets with a total of 1,548 bomber and 1,111 fighter sorties. The I.Jagdkorps formed two Gefechtsverbanden, one over Magdeburg consisting of I. and II./JG 300 and the other over the Müritz See, north of Berlin, consisting of III./JG 300 and II./ZG 26. The Magdeburg Gefechtsverband hit the 3rd Bomb Division, claiming five B-17s and two P-51 fighters while losing six Bf 109 fighters.

A total of 245 B-24 bombers of the 2nd Bomb Division reached the Pölitz synthetic fuel plant, via a northern route over Denmark. The division was badly spread out by the time it reached the target area. For about four minutes, the formation was only covered by a single fighter group. The III./JG 300 hit the rear of the 44th Bomb Group, but was attacked by escorting fighters that shot down 13 Bf 109 fighters. However, this left the neighboring 492nd Bomb Group exposed, and it was attacked by Me 410 heavy fighters of ZG 26. The 856th Bomb Squadron on the left of the group formation was the most heavily hit. Nine of their eleven bombers were shot down before reaching the target area; two of their damaged bombers escaped to Sweden. Not a single bomber from the squadron returned to base. P-51s finally intervened, and ZG 26 had 12 of their heavy fighters shot down or crashed while landing. ZG 26 claimed 36 bomber kills that day; total 2nd Bomb Division casualties were 34 including those that were interned in Sweden.

The Pölitz synthetic fuel plant had previously been struck on May 29; the return raid on June 20 was effective in preventing the plant from re-opening production after extensive repair work. This would become a pattern in the Oil Campaign. Major plants such as Pölitz would be struck at intervals to smash up any reconstruction.

Sometimes dubbed "The Bottisham Four," this is a formation of P-51D fighters of the 375th Squadron, 361st Fighter Group taken on July 26 or 27, 1944, flying from RAF Bottisham. The aircraft in the foreground is an early P-51D-5-NA, (44-13410, code E2-C) named "Lou IV" and flown by the group commander, Col. Thomas J J Christian. He was shot down and killed on August 12,1944 near Boisleux-au-Mont, France.

Many of the heavy bomber missions in late June 1944 were directed against tactical targets in France including railyards, V-weapon storage areas, and other targets. In some cases, for example Mission 438 on June 24, the bomb divisions had separate targets on that day; five bomb wings of the 1st and 3rd Bomb Divisions attacked oil targets in the Bremen area. Of the 340 bombers dispatched, 213 bombers reached the targets. Bombing was done using Pathfinders due to cloud cover. Because of the weather, the I.Jagdkorps made no effort to intercept the mission. Mission 447 on June 29 was a combined effort in the Leipzig area mainly directed against aircraft plants. It included a raid on the Bohlen synthetic fuel plant by 81 B-17s of the 3rd Bomb Division.

There was no Luftwaffe response to the June 29 raid. This was in part due to weather, but also due to the declining number of operational aircraft and crews. At the end of June 1944, Luftflotte Reich had only 254 operational day-fighters compared to 643 at the end of March 1944.

The first raid on oil facilities in July was Mission 458 on July 7. This included 2nd Bomb Division attacks on Lützkendorf and Halle, 3rd Bomb Division on Böhlen and Merseberg,

A formation of Boeing B-17Gs of the 532nd Bomb Squadron, 381st Bomb Group on a mission during the late summer of 1944. The aircraft in the center is B-17G-65-BO "Trudie's Terror" (43-37675), and behind is B-17G-35-DL "Sleepy Time Gal" (42-107112).

Rocket defenders of Leuna

The first Me 163 Komet rocket-fighter squadron was based at Brandis in order to protect the vital Leuna chemical complex. They began to see combat action against the Eighth Air Force in late August 1944. On August 24, the Staffel had one of its largest commitments to date, putting eight of the tiny rocket fighters in the air. The usual tactic was for the fighters to use their high acceleration to fly over the bomber formations. They could then use their rocket motors to descend rapidly through the bomber formation, or switch off their motor to conserve fuel and glide through the American bombers. The two 30mm MK 108 cannon were lethal against bombers, but getting a hit on the bombers during a fast descent proved to be very difficult. That day, Feldwebel Schubert claimed to have shot down two B-17s northwest of Leipzig at 1208–1209, while Leutnant Bott claimed to have shot a B-17 out of formation at roughly the same location a few moments later.

and the 1st Bomb Division against two facilities in the Leipzig area. In contrast to the previous two oil raids, this mission was heavily contested by the I.Jagdkorps.

The 1. and 7.Jagddivsion were instructed to form Gefechtsverbanden over the Leipzig area. A new Sturmgruppe, IV.(Sturm)/JG 3 had become fully operational and had their deadly combat debut that day. These were equipped with the upgraded Fw 190A-8/R2 Sturmbock fighters.

The 1.Jagddivision control center ordered its formations to attack the third wing on the northern side of the bomber stream, the 14th Combat Wing. The nearest German fighter force consisted of 42 Me 410 heavy fighters of ZG 26, escorted by 37 Bf 109 fighters from III./JG 300. The Bf 109s suffered heavily from the intervention of escort fighters, losing 13 Bf 109s while claiming only one P-51 and two B-24s. The Me 410s claimed four B-24 bombers but lost eight aircraft in the process. This was followed by an attack by II./JG 5, the other two Gruppen of JG 300 as well as its Stab, along with 44 of the Fw 190 Sturmbock assault fighters. The I./JG 300, assigned to deal with the escort fighters, was scattered by the Flak before being struck by the P-51s. The Gruppe claimed five bombers and two P-51s for the loss of nine Bf 109s. The Stabschwarm and II./JG 300 struck the 14th Combat Wing from the other side. They claimed 28 B-24s from their attack.

Their attack was followed by the IV.(Sturm)/JG 3. They pummeled the hapless 492nd Bomb Group, which had suffered heavily a month before during the first attack on the Pölitz plant. A total of 11 B-24s from this group were lost, plus eight more from the other two squadrons, at a cost of four Fw 190s. The 1.Jagdkorps claimed 81 victories on June 7, with JG 300 claiming 34 and IV.(Sturm)/JG 3 claiming 22. The air battle became a sensation in the German press, touted as the "Lightning air battle over Oschersleben." In reality, the kill claims were significantly overstated. The 2nd Bomb Division suffered the heaviest losses of 28 bombers while the other two divisions lost nine more. Escort fighter losses were six, for a grand total of 43, about half the German claims. Furthermore, some of the USAAF losses were due to Flak and at least two to aerial collisions. The USAAF was no stranger to exaggerated claims, with the bombers claiming 39 enemy fighters and the escort fighters another 75.

The fighter inspector, Adolf Galland, saw the battle over Oschersleben as a vindication of his support for the Sturmgruppe concept. Following the June 7 battle, he began pushing to expand the existing force from one to three Sturmguppen. The USAAF described the new tactics as a "Company Front" but it took some time to realize that its effectiveness depended on the heavily armored Sturmbock fighters as well the lethality of the new 30mm cannon.

In spite of ecstatic German press reaction to the July 7 battle, German leaders were less optimistic. The bombing raids had reduced German liquid fuel production from 1,645 tonnes daily to 600 tonnes. Production would begin to rebound during the second week of June only to collapse late in the month due to continuing USAAF and RAF attacks.

The next major Oil Campaign was Mission 484 on July 20 as part of a package of strikes on a variety of oil and industrial targets in western and southwestern Germany. The 1st Bomb Division was hit by the 7.Jagddivision Gefechtsverband. The German fighters claimed 29 kills during the day's fighting with JG 300 claiming 20 and the Sturmgruppe of JG 3 claiming three. Actual losses were 15 B-17 in the 1st Bomb Division, one B-24 from the 2nd Bomb Division and eight escort fighters. Although the attacks were not on the scale of the June 7 mission, the bombers managed to smash up several synthetic fuel plants on the verge of recovering from previous attacks. German daily fuel production fell from 1,380 tonnes to 120 tonnes. This attack was followed by the last oil mission of the month, Mission 501 on July 28. This raid included 766 bombers of the 1st and 3rd Bomb Division against the Leuna and Leipzig synthetic plants. Luftwaffe defense efforts were very weak, in part due to the commitment of JG 300 against a Fifteenth Air Force mission in the Budapest area. It was noteworthy in that the first German Me 163 rocket fighter was spotted that day. The Leuna facility was put "entirely out of action" for the time being according to an Ultra decrypt.

August Oil Campaign

The Oil Campaign resumed on August 4 with three days of successive missions that included a wide range of industrial targets including some oil refineries. Mission 514 on August 4 was oriented towards the north including the Bremen area and a deep mission to Peenemunde. The Sturm Staffel of JG 3 attempted to intercept but ran out of fuel and returned to base. Five other Gruppen sent fighters but they were hit by escorting USAAF fighters, losing 29 fighters for the meager result of one bomber and two escort fighters; nearly all of the bomber losses were due to Flak.

A similar set of objectives, but in central Germany, was the objective the following day. Mission 519 on August 5 saw relatively light activity by the I.Jagdkorps with Luftwaffe fighters claiming five of the 13 bombers shot down; escort fighters claim to have shot down 29 German fighters. Mission 524 on August 6 hit targets in the Brandenberg and Hamburg areas and losses included 24 bombers and eight escort fighters. Most of these were due to Flak or other causes. The I.Jagdkorps managed to sortie 198 fighters of which 128 made contact. Of these, 30 were shot down and JG 300 claimed only four bomber kills that day. A German report described the day's activities as a complete failure.

For the next week, the bombers were heavily involved in missions over France to assist in the Allied breakout operations in Normandy. A number of raids on oil refineries were conducted in the middle of August, though few dedicated primarily to fuel targets. The only major Oil Campaign raid was Mission 556 on August 16 involving 976 bombers and 612 fighters. The I.Jagdkorps managed to get 121 fighters aloft, including all five Me 163 rocket fighters of 1./JG 400. It's worth noting that this Staffel was specifically deployed to the Brandis air base to defend the Leipzig fuel plants, including the massive Leuna complex. Two of the new rocket fighters were lost, one to B-17 gunners and one to a P-51 of the 359th Fighter Group. The Me 163 fighters were credited with three "shot-out-of-formation"

A storm of Flak greets the B-17G bombers of the 3rd Bomb Division during Mission 570 over the Pölitz synthetic fuel plants on August 25, 1945.

victories though in fact none of the B-17s were actually shot down. Other claims were ten B-17s, mainly by JG 302, and three P-51 Mustangs. Escort fighters claimed to have shot down 32 German fighters.

The Oil Campaign resumed on August 24 with Mission 568 including many familiar synthetic fuel targets such as Brüx, Misburg, Stade, and Leuna/Merseburg. The I.Jagdkorps put 222 fighters in the air but only 99 made interceptions. The Gefechtsverband intercepted the 1st Bomb Division in the Lüneburg area claiming ten B-17s destroyed and seven more shot-out-of-formation or destroyed stragglers; actual losses were 16 to all causes. The Me 163 fighters returned to combat, with the largest commitment to date of eight rocket fighters. Feldwebel Schubert claimed to have shot down two B-17s northwest of Leipzig at 1208–1209, while Leutnant Bott of the same Staffel claimed to have shot a B-17 out of formation at roughly the location a few moments later. The Me 163 fighters also dueled with escorting P-51 fighters, but without results.

The following day, Mission 570 again went east, aimed at aircraft plants, the Peenemunde and Rechnlin test facilities, and a few synthetic fuel plants, notably Pölitz. Deep missions such as this one usually attracted Luftwaffe fighters, but once again, fighter resistance was extremely weak. Luftwaffe fighters claimed only one aerial victory, JG 53 shooting down a P-38 escort fighter. Two fighter Gruppen that had been transferred back from France for Reich defense had a very bad day. The III./JG 76 lost 11 killed including its commander; II./JG 6 lost 19 killed and four wounded and its commander was subsequently relieved of duty for the group's appalling performance. The latter unit was based around a cadre of Zerstörer pilots who had been transferred to Fw 190 fighters without adequate training and with little knowledge of single-seat fighter tactics. American bomber losses were due primarily to Flak. This was the last major Oil Campaign mission of August, due to the return of cloudy conditions over Germany as well as the demands of the Allied ground campaign.

Besides the attacks on the synthetic fuel plants, the Oil Campaign also was directed against fuel storage facilities and oil refineries. Of the 60 raids in August, only a quarter were against synthetic fuel plants while half were against storage and a quarter against refineries.

Although Auschwitz is most notorious for its role as a death camp, IG Farben erected its Buna-Werke for the production of synthetic rubber and fuel at Auschwitz III-Monowitz (Oświęcim-Monowice), a subsidiary camp about six kilometers from the main camp. This is an image of a B-17G during the first air strike by the Fifteenth Air Force against the IG Farben plant on August 20, 1944.

Ploesti subdued

On June 8, Spaatz informed the Fifteenth Air Force that their number one priority would be the destruction of the Romanian oil refineries. The summer campaign against Ploesti was a grinding, attritional struggle. There was no longer any illusion that the extensive fuel infrastructure could be destroyed by a few pin-point attacks. By the early summer of 1944, half of the sixty oil refineries in Romania and Hungary had been damaged or destroyed.

The Luftwaffe and FAAR (*Forțele Aeriene Regale Române:* Royal Romanian Air Force) were directed by the Jagdfliegerführer Balkan. In the early summer, these units were still relatively robust, for example conducting 198 fighter sorties against the June 23 mission. However, the growing force of escort fighters assigned to the Fifteenth Air Force took a heavy toll on these forces. During the June 23 air battles, USAAF escort fighters claimed 24 German and Romanian fighters around Ploesti, including the loss of two of four of the Romanian group commanders. In late June 1944, the Fifteenth Fighter Command changed its tactics, to conform to those already being used by the Eighth Air Force. A portion of the escort fighters were diverted to sweeps against the Romanian and German airfields. The strength of the German and Romanian fighter units declined steadily. By late July, less than 50 fighters were active on a daily basis.

The main threat to the bombers was Ploesti's formidable Flak defenses. The 142 heavy Flak guns available in April 1944 increased to 253 guns by the summer of 1944, all concentrated in an area only about 12 x 16 miles (19 x 26km). Most of the 105mm and 128mm guns were rail-mobile on special platforms, permitting them to be shifted around the city where needed. The Flak batteries were provided with ample supplies of ammunition. The Ploesti defenses still managed to inflict surprisingly heavy losses on occasion. For example, on the night of August 9, the RAF's 205 Group staged a night mission with 61 Wellington, Liberator, and Halifax bombers, losing 11 bombers to Flak and Axis night-fighters, nearly a fifth of the force. Passive Luftwaffe defenses such as smoke generators degraded the accuracy of the bombers.

When not bombing Ploesti, the Fifteenth Air Force often attacked oil targets in Hungary, Austria, and Poland. For example, on July 10, the two refineries near Vienna were hit,

A formation of B-17Gs of the Fifteenth Air Force bombing rail and oil targets in the Debrecen, Hungary area on September 21, 1944. After the capture of the Ploesti oil fields in August, the Hungarian oil fields were the last major source of imported fuel for the Wehrmacht.

shutting down production for at least four weeks and destroying several hundred thousand tonnes of petrol in nearby storage facilities.

FIFTEENTH AIR FORCE PLOESTI MISSIONS, 1944						
	B-17 sorties*	B-24 sorties*	Total	Tonnage on target	Bomber losses	Escort Fighter losses
5 Apr 44	94	136	230	587.3	13	2
15 Apr 44	137	43	180	316.4	3	
24 Apr 44	154	136	290	793.5	8	3
5 May 44	166	319	485	1,256.5	19	1
18 May 44	33	173	206	493	14	2
31 May 44	53	428	481	1,115.6	16	4
6 Jun 44		310	310	697.5	14	
10 Jun 44	38**		38	18.5	10	14
23 Jun 44	139		139	283.2		7
24 Jun 44		135	135	329	14	1
9 Jul 44	122	109	231	605	1	
15 Jul 44	153	451	604	1,480.7	20	2
22 Jul 44	132	327	459	1,234.7	25	3
28 Jul 44	102	222	324	841.7	20	5
31 Jul 44	154		154	434.7	2	
10 Aug 44	124	218	342	780.4	15	1
17 Aug 44		245	245	534.2	19	1
18 Aug 44	148	125	273	628.5	7	
19 Aug 44	65		65	144.2	2	1
Total	1,814+38**	3,377	5,229	12,717	222	47

*Only effective sorties are tallied; aircraft returning to base and failing to bomb not counted
**P-38 attack

The 1944 air campaign against Ploesti reduced but did not shut off the Romanian supply of refined petroleum to Germany. Refined fuel production at Ploesti had totaled 269,000 tonnes monthly prior to the 1944 bombing campaign. By May, it fell to 120,000 tonnes and by August to 84,000 tonnes. By early August 1944, the Ploesti refinery system had been shattered and the loss of infrastructure had made it nearly impossible to ship their petroleum products to Germany. As can be seen on the accompanying chart, only a fraction of the Ploesti output could actually be shipped to Germany due to the destruction of the rail and river transportation network. The final four raids were staged on August 17–19, shortly before the capture of Ploesti by the Red Army.

FUEL EXPORTS FROM ROMANIA (IN THOUSANDS OF TONNES)			
Month	Total crude oil throughput	Aviation gasoline to Luftwaffe	Gasoline to the Wehrmacht
Dec 43	419	15	68
Apr 44	173	8	35
May 44	162	8	26
Jun 44	78	2	17
Jul 44	184	7	20
Aug 44	122	0.3	12

From April to August 1944, there were a total of 6,564 bomber sorties of which 5,229 reached and bombed their objectives. In addition, RAF bombers conducted three night-missions on June 26–27, August 9–10, and August 17–18 totaling 186 sorties, and dropping 313 tons of bombs at a cost of 19 bombers. Romania pulled out of the war in late August and the Red Army captured Ploesti on August 29, 1944.

Summer assessment

The August Oil Campaign had crippled the German synthetic fuel plants. Hardest hit was aviation fuel production which fell from the April total of 175,000 tonnes to only 12,000 tonnes. To put this in some perspective, in May 1944 Luftwaffe fighter units involved in the defense of the Reich consumed 195,000 tonnes of aviation fuel. Production of gasoline/petrol was reduced from 125,000 tonnes to 60,000 tonnes. Diesel fuel was reduced from 89,000 tonnes to 65,000 tonnes. Speer warned Hitler that "The possibility of moving troops at the front will be so restricted that planned operations in October will no longer be able to take place. With this fuel situation, offensive operations will be impossible."

Not only had the synthetic fuel plants been ruined, but Romania had been forced out of the war in late August, cutting off Germany's primary source for imported oil products. Even after the substantial growth of the German synthetic fuel industry during the war years, Romania had been providing Germany with about a quarter of its liquid fuel.

On August 10, the *Oberkommando Luftwaffe* (OKL: Luftwaffe High Command) ordered a general curtailment of operational flight activity except for fighter defense due to the growing fuel shortage. Reconnaissance was to be flown only when absolutely essential; bomber

A P-38 named "Dossie" of the 479th Fighter Group based at Wattisham, England. The 479th was the last fighter group to join the Eighth Air Force in May 1944. Known as "Riddle's Raiders," the group converted to the P-51 in the fall of 1944.

operations required special permission from Berlin. On August 13, Berlin ordered the conversion of all Wehrmacht supply vehicles to producer gas (vehicle fuel using techniques such as wood or coal burning converters) by October 1 in order to save petrol/gasoline for tanks and combat vehicles. Ultra decrypts of Kriegsmarine radio traffic in mid-August indicated that Berlin expected that fuel stocks would not last more than six months if the current situation continued.

In his August 30 report to Hitler, Speer also warned that the attack on the synthetic fuel plants would cripple other aspects of German war production. The synthetic plants were responsible for the manufacture of a substantial portion of other critical industrial chemicals including methanol, nitrogen products, and artificial rubber. Methanol was used in the production of key explosives including Hexogen and TNT as well as the production of industrial resins and plastics. Nitrogen was a key ingredient in high explosives. Speer warned Hitler that military explosive production could receive priority for nitrogen production. But that would mean that production of nitrogen-based fertilizers for agriculture would have to be cut back or halted, probably leading to food shortages.

From the Luftwaffe perspective, the summer 1944 campaigns had been a catastrophe. At the end of August 1944, the nine fighter Gruppen of I.Jagdkorps had been battered down to a paltry 89 fighters. The command-and-control infrastructure of the Reich defense force had been badly disrupted by the collapse of the Wehrmacht in France and Belgium. The network of forward-alert radars along the French and Belgian coast were now gone, leading to a massive gap in early-warning coverage. Luftflotte 3 had suffered heavy losses in its fighter units and had been pushed back to German soil with

P-47D (42-27339, code MX-S) of the 82nd Squadron, 78th Fighter Group seen at Bassingbourn in the autumn of 1944 after its usual airfield at Duxford was flooded. This aircraft was flown by Lt. Col. Joseph Myers and was credited with downing the first Me 262 jet on August 28, 1944, piloted by Oberfeldwebel Hieronymous Lauer of I./KG 51. Laurer was credited with seven and a half victories during the war.

the exception of a few forward-deployed units in the Netherlands. It was redesignated as *Luftwaffenkommando West* (Air Command West) on 26 September 1944. On top of this, the Allied advance to the German frontier meant that the Allied tactical air forces were now rampaging in German air-space. The Reich defense force now had to face daily incursions by Allied fighters, fighter-bombers, and medium bombers. Luftwaffe air bases in western Germany frequently came under attack by roving Allied aircraft. Germany was no longer a safe haven for Luftwaffe training schools. This resulted in the "massacre of the children" when many young pilot cadets were shot down during training flights.

The Luftwaffe Reich defense force, although allotted the highest priority for new pilots, suffered from continual shortages starting in the summer of 1944. Fuel supplies to the elementary training units was almost entirely cut off in July 1944 due to the growing fuel shortages brought about by the Oil Campaign. The priority given to fighter production led to a shortage of primary trainers such as the Ar 96. A portion of these schools were closed and their instructor pilots transferred to fighter units. To make up for the shortage of new pilots and a lack of fuel, numerous non-fighter units were grounded including bomber, reconnaissance, and transport units. Their pilots were given a hasty operational conversion courses and sent off to the fighter units.

Not only was there a continual shortage of new fighter pilots, but the quality of the new pilots continually deteriorated. The new pilots seldom received enough blind flying training, which may not seem like a major issue for day-fighters, but in fact, the training was so limited that these new pilots were not competent to fly on cloudy days since they readily became lost. Up to the end of 1943, German fighter pilots usually had about 20 hours of operational flight time on an actual fighter aircraft before being sent into action. By 1944, new pilots were often sent on their first combat missions without the luxury of operational training. In many cases, these novice pilots were a greater threat to themselves than to the American bombers.

At least on paper, Speer's fighter program had significantly increased fighter production, peaking in September 1944 at 3,031 new fighters compared to only 1,316 in January 1944. There is some suspicion that these numbers were artificially inflated to placate Hitler. A post-war US Air Force assessment suggested that fighters sent back to the factories for repair, and new fighters sent to Luftwaffe depots for armament upgrades, were issued new *Werknummern* (serial numbers), and hence recounted as "new" production. The increase in fighter production came at the expense of other aircraft types, as well as a reduction in the manufacture of spare parts. Bomber production was sharply curtailed. Due to increased fighter production, the I.Jagdkorps saw a significant rebuilding of strength in September, even if the quality of its aircrews was depressingly poor.

Horst Wessel over the Baltic

By the summer of 1944, the Me 410 heavy fighter was less than ideal for the bomber interception mission. It was simply too slow and unmaneuverable to survive against the USAAF escort fighters. By the spring of 1944, the tactic of attacking the bombers from the rear using rockets was abandoned since the rocket tubes significantly degraded the Me 410's performance. Instead, various cannon upgrades were used to enhance the lethality of the Me 410 against bombers such as the Me 410B-2/U2/R4 seen here. The "U" suffix indicated Umrüst-Bausätze, factory conversion kits while the "R" identified the Rüstsätze armament upgrade. Although the MK 103 30mm cannon was a preferred option, shortage of these weapons led to the use on this version of two 7.92mm MG 17 machine guns and two 13mm MG 131 machine guns in the nose, plus two 20mm MG 151 cannons in a pannier under the fuselage.

In spite of their shortcomings, the Me 410 could be deadly when it caught the bombers without their escorts. On June 20, II./ZG 26 "Horst Wessel" hit the 492nd Bomb Group and other elements of the 2nd Bomber Division over the Baltic, claiming 36 bomber kills. P-51s intervened later, and ZG 26 had 12 of their heavy fighters shot down or crashed while landing.

The Fall 1944 Oil Campaign

The Oil Campaign in September 1944 was disrupted by both operational considerations as well as weather. Eisenhower requested the use of heavy bombers to assist in moving crucial fuel supplies to the armies along the German border due to the poor state of the French and Belgian railways caused by the persistent Allied bombing. Operation *Market-Garden*, the airborne operation against the Rhine bridges in the Netherlands, further diverted bomber missions.

However, the main impediment was the onset of the autumn rainy season which was unusually wet in 1944. Although the Eighth Air Force could use Pathfinder techniques and the H2X radar to bomb through the cloud cover, this was invariably less accurate than visual bombing. Under 10/10 cloud cover, only 0.2 percent of the bombs fell within 1,000 feet of the aiming point; less than half fell within three miles. At 5/10 cloud cover, about 4.4 percent fell within 1,000 feet and about a half within one mile. In general, the Eighth Air Force scheduled oil missions whenever the weather over Germany was expected to be wholly or partially clear. Due to fluctuating weather conditions and incorrect forecast, missions fell back on PFF (Pathfinder Force) tactics if the target was obscured.

The first major raid in September was Mission 605. There was no German fighter response and two B-17s were lost to Flak. A return attack was made on Mission 611 on September 8, once again without Luftwaffe fighters appearing.

The first substantial September attack was Mission 623 on September 11 involving all three bomb divisions totaling 1,016 bombers and 411 escort fighters. This led to a massive Luftwaffe response including virtually every unit of I.Jagdkorps, and even a large portion

A Fifteenth Air Force B-24 is seen over the Nyíregyháza marshalling yards in Hungary on a mission on September 6, 1944. These transportation targets were complementary to the oil targets, intended to shut off the flow of Hungarian oil to Germany.

of II.Jagdkorps, the tactical fighter force in western Germany under Luftkommando West. About four hundred fighters sortied, though only 305 German fighters actually engaged the bomber streams. The 1./JG 400 put up seven Me 163 fighters and claimed to have shot down one bomber. Although USAAF losses were significant – 40 bombers and 17 escort fighters – Luftwaffe losses were horrific. About 110 fighters were shot down or damaged beyond repair or more than a third of the attacking force. The USAAF escort fighters claimed 115 German fighters in the air and 42 on the ground. A total of 60 German pilots were killed and 25 wounded.

The weather remained favorable the following day, so the Eighth Air Force staged Mission 626 against the same array of oil targets in central Germany with 813 bombers and 579 escort fighters. Due to the previous day's losses, the I.Jagdkorps put up only about half as many fighters with about 190 sorties. Three Gefechtsverbanden were formed. The first, based around the II.(Sturm)/JG 4 with escorts from other units, struck the 1st Bomb Division on the approach over Magdeburg. This unit claimed 27 B-17s and 2 P-51s but actual losses were only 19 B-17s. German losses were significant, losing 13 Bf 109s and 7 Fw 190s as well as 16 pilots killed and 4 wounded. The Sturmgruppe commander, Major von Kornatzki was one of the casualties.

The largest Gefectsverband was based around JG 300 and hit the American bomber stream closer to the target areas, north of Berlin. The 3rd Bomb Division was heaviest hit by these attacks, losing 12 B-17 bombers including a few to Flak. The final Gefechtsverband made up from the II.Jagdkorps hit the bomber stream during the withdrawal phase. These groups

A B-17G from the 3rd Bomb Division can be seen over the IG Farben synthetic fuel plant in Ludwigshafen after it was bombed on September 13, 1944 during Mission 628. A total of 74 B-17s took part in the raid, dropping 212 tons of bombs.

P-51B-15-NA "The Iowa Beaut" flown by Lt Kevin G Rafferty of the 354th Squadron, 355th Fighter Group. This aircraft was lost on Mission 623 on September 11, 1944 while escorting the 2nd Bomb Division to Madgeburg. It crashed in Hörnsheim, near Wetzlar and was probably the victim of a Me 262A-1 flown by Ofw. Helmut Baudach of Epr. Kdo. 262, the jet operational conversion unit.

were unaccustomed to being confronted by such a large force of escort fighters and lost 29 Fw 190s, 14 pilots killed, and 13 wounded while only shooting down two P-51s. Once again, the day's losses on the German side were catastrophic. Of the 147 fighters to attack the USAAF formations, 76 were shot down, or more than half the force. A total of 42 pilots were killed and 14 injured. USAAF losses were 35 bombers and 14 fighters.

Due to favorable weather, the Eighth Air Force struck again on September 13 with 790 bombers reaching their targets, escorted by 542 fighters. The I.Jagdkorps had suffered such heavy losses in the two previous days that it could only conduct 137 sorties, mainly by JG 300. The German fighters were grossly outnumbered and their formations were broken up. Only 63 actually took part in the air battles. They claimed 4 bombers of 15 lost that day, and 4 fighters of the 10 lost. The escort fighters claimed 33 aerial victories and 25 aircraft on the ground.

As a result of the catastrophic losses suffered by I.Jagdkorps in three days of fighting, a special meeting was held with Hitler and Göring including all the major unit commanders. There was considerable bickering between various officers about the proper anti-bomber tactics. Hitler had not been told that one of his pet projects, the Me 410 with 5cm cannon, had been withdrawn from combat due to its poor performance. He took the news with surprising equanimity given his usual tendencies. After being briefed on the situation, he gave the fighter pilots one concession they had been seeking since early summer. Until then, the new Me 262 jet had been allotted to KG 51 as a fighter-bomber. Now, Hitler agreed that it would be used for defense of the Reich in a fighter role.

The III./ZG 26 had provided much of the staff for the Me 262 operational training units and so it was reformed as III./JG 6 to receive the new Me 262 fighters. From the experience

of KG 51, the Me 262 was most vulnerable to Allied fighters during take-off and landing. As a result, the III./JG 54, equipped with the new Fw 190D-9 fighter, was assigned to provide air cover over the Me 262 bases.

The I.Jagdkorps did not return to battle until September 27 when the Eighth Air Force staged Mission 650 against targets in western Germany along the Rhine. The bomber mission was frustrated by cloud cover, but the 445th Bomb Group became separated from the rest of the formation without escort. This was immediately spotted by Luftwaffe controllers who directed three Sturmgruppen to attack. This force numbered 121 fighters including the associated Bf 109 escorts. The Sturmgruppe attacked in three waves of about 15 fighters each. In about five minutes, 25 B-24s were shot down and 5 more crash landed in France or England; only 7 emerged unscathed. Although this reinforced the reputation of the Sturmbock formations, losses were still painfully heavy – 25 Fw 190s and 5 Bf 109s along with 18 pilots killed and 8 wounded.

The Eighth Air Force returned to its usual oil targets in central Germany on Mission 652 on September 28. The I.Jagdkorps could only put 96 fighters in the air that day due to the previous day's losses. Of these, six were Me 163 rocket fighters protecting the Leuna works. They were largely ineffective with only one entering combat without results. Once again, the Sturmgruppen were the centerpiece of the German attacks, waiting until there was a gap in escort coverage to attack. The 303rd Bomb Group lost 11 B-17s and the 457th lost seven before escort fighters arrived back on scene. This was the last mission for Eighth Air Force's P-38 fighters, with the squadrons completing their transition to P-51D fighters. Overall US casualties were 34 bombers and 7 fighters with claims of 10 German fighters by the bomber crews and 26 by the fighter crews.

Although "Bomber Harris" continued to deride oil objectives as "panacea targets," pressure from Churchill, Portal, and Tedder forced him to follow the new post-*Overlord* priorities. The first major RAF Oil Campaign mission in September 1944 was a daylight mission on

Halifaxes of No. 466 Squadron RAAF, 4 Group being prepared at RAF Driffield for a mission against German synthetic fuel plants in the Ruhr in September 1944. (AWM)

A Halifax III (LL590, code Z5-E) of No. 462 Squadron RAAF, 4 Group based at RAF Driffield flies over the English countryside during a September 1944 mission. (AWM)

September 11 by 205 Halifaxes, 154 Lancasters, and 20 Mosquitoes against the usual oil targets in western Germany including Castrop-Rauxel and Gelsenkirchen. The bombers were escorted by 26 squadrons of Spitfires, Mustangs, and Tempests. The Luftwaffe made no effort to intervene and the six bombers lost on the mission fell victim to Flak or accidental bomb strikes from other aircraft. The attacks resumed the following day against other synthetic fuel plants with 315 Halifaxes, 75 Lancasters, and 22 Mosquitoes. Losses were seven bombers, once again due to Flak since there was no German fighter response. Gelsenkirchen was revisited on September 13 by 102 Halifaxes, 28 Lancasters, and 10 Mosquitoes with 2 Halifaxes lost. On September 25, the British Air Staff sent a directive to Harris that the Oil Campaign was the first priority after a series of the usual sort of night raids on German cities in mid-September. Harris responded with a September 27 mission against Bottrop and Sterkrade with 346 aircraft. No aircraft were lost on either mission. Both targets were the subject of another attack on September 30 by 275 aircraft but cloud cover over the target meant that only a small portion of the force hit the synthetic plants while the others attacked targets-of-opportunity.

September had been a very bad month for the German fuel industry and the Luftwaffe. In late August, Speer reported to Hitler that he hoped that repair work would permit the production of 22,200 tonnes of aviation fuel, but in the event it had produced only 9,400 tonnes. This was only 5 percent of the level of production in April 1944 before the Oil Campaign had started. The situation with other fuels was equally bleak, and Speer warned that the reliable supply of coal to the Ruhr, needed not only for synthetic fuel but also many other industrial applications, had fallen to a single month's stockpile.

October missions

Weather delayed Eighth Air Force raids until October 7 with Mission 669 against the usual cluster of synthetic plants in central and northern Germany. There were 1,401 bombers and 521 fighters involved. The I.Jagdkorps had still not recovered from the September debacle, and had lost 17 fighters the day before during a USAAF mission near Berlin. A total of seven Jagdgruppen took part in the day's fighting with 113 sorties of which 80 reached the combat area. A total of 12 B-17s of the 3rd Bomb Division were shot down near Leipzig after nearly all of the German fighters had formed a concentrated Gefechtsverband. The ensuing fights with the escort fighters led to the loss of 16 German fighters, nine pilots killed and three wounded. Three Me 163 fighters were lost that day, two of them to ground accidents. The highest scoring Me 163 pilot, Fw. Siegfried Schubert, was among those killed when his fighter crashed due to an accident with the take-off trolley.

This mission also resulted in the first contact during the Oil Campaign with the new Me 262 fighter unit, III./JG 6. The Gruppe was based at Achmer in northwestern Germany within easy range of the "Bomber autobahn." But it was also close enough to the Dutch border that it fell in range of not only Allied escort fighters, but also tactical fighters. The jet fighters were under instructions from Berlin to avoid attacking the bombers due to a lack of armored protection. Nevertheless, three pilots claimed to have shot down B-24s though only two claims were accepted. The US crews insisted that no bombers were lost to the new fighters. Two fighters were shot down during the engagement and two more were shot down while taking off from their base at Achmer.

Due to the dramatically reduced threat of Luftwaffe day-fighters, the RAF began to conduct missions into the Ruhr during daylight. This is a Halifax of 6 Group during a mission to the Wanne-Eickel synthetic fuel plant on October 12, 1944.

A B-24J of the Fifteenth Air Force trails smoke after passing through heavy Flak over Vienna on a mission in October 1944. Oil targets in the Vienna area attacked in October included the Lobau and Schwechat oil refineries and Winterhafen oil depot.

The I.Jagdkorps, now down to under a hundred ready fighters, did not contest the Eighth Air Force oil attacks on October 11 through the middle of the month. The Ruhr oil plants, usually the objectives of RAF Bomber Command, were struck by a large mission on October 25 without a Luftwaffe response. Indeed, the bombers hardly ever saw the I.Jagdkorps again in October in part due to the heavy losses and in part due to the arrival of autumn cloud cover. The Fifteenth Air Force flying from Italy continued its attacks into central Europe with four raids, including a major mission to Brüx.

RAF Bomber Command continued its daylight missions against synthetic fuel plants in the Ruhr starting on October 6. Of the 220 bombers on the mission, nine were lost, all due to Flak. A raid by 137 Halifaxes and Lancasters of 6 and 8 Group on October 12 at Wanne-Eickel did little damage to the refinery since a storage tank hit early in the raid obscured the target with dense smoke. A neighboring chemical plant was severely damaged. The Homberg synthetic fuel plant was revisited on October 25 by 243 bombers of 6 and 8 Group. There were two more raids late in the month on October 30 and 31 against Wesseling and Bottorp, both of which had to be conducted with navigation aids due to cloud cover.

In spite of explicit Air Staff directives, Harris continued to show little enthusiasm for the Oil Campaign. Only 6 percent of the October missions, 3,653 tons, had been directed against oil targets compared to 74 percent in the "Third Battle of the Ruhr" directed against a number of cities and towns. Even the official RAF history noted that "the enemy this month had a chance to repair the refineries which had been so battered in the second week of September." Tedder had become frustrated with Harris's obstinate refusal to take sufficient action, and on November 1, the Air Staff, with the backing of the Combined Chiefs of

Staff, issued yet another directive listing oil and transportation in its most explicit rejection yet of Bomber Command's concentration on area-bombing of cities. Harris threatened to resign over the issue, which was rebuffed by Portal due to the impact it would have had on Bomber Command morale.

The November reprieve

The only time that the German fuel industry showed a slight recovery was during the month of November 1944. This was in large measure due to weather. Cloud cover frequently obscured the target areas, degrading the performance of the Eighth Air Force's day missions by forcing the use of less accurate radar-directed bombing. Only 10.1 percent of the bombs delivered in October–November 1944 were visually aimed compared to 41.5 percent in the previous spring and summer months. In addition, the onset of the shorter number of daylight hours during the autumn made long-range missions to eastern Germany more difficult. The Fifteenth Air Force had particular difficulties in operating over the Alps during this season.

The Eighth Air Force returned to attack the Ruhr synthetic plants due to Harris's reluctance to press the Oil Campaign. Mission 696 on November 1 hit Gelsenkirchen, but had to be conducted using H2X radar due to cloud cover. There was no Luftwaffe fighter resistance. Mission 698 on November 2 was staged against Leuna/Merseberg as well as some of the Ruhr plants. After avoiding contact for the last two weeks of October, I.Jagdkorps showed up in force that day with 490 sorties. While weather interfered with USAAF operations, it also interfered with Luftwaffe fighter operations, and about a quarter of the day's Luftwaffe sorties were unable to find the bombers.

The Me 262 fighters of III./JG 6 had been modified with new WG 21 rocket launchers under their nose in the hopes of making them more effective against the bombers. A total of six of the jet fighters sortied from Achmer and tried to use the new weapons without success. One fighter managed to damage a P-47 with cannon fire, but that was the Gruppe's only contribution to the day's fighting.

A Lancaster of 460 Squadron RAAF (code AR-P), 1 Group being bombed up for a mission at RAF Binbrook, in Lincolnshire in July 1944. This aircraft is probably NE141, piloted by PO R. F. McMaster, that was lost over Aschaffenburg on November 22, 1944. (Australian War Memorial)

The "Bungay Buckaroos," the 446th Bomb Group on Mission 723 on November 25, 1944 against the Leuna synthetic fuel plant and other targets. The aircraft in the foreground is a B-24H-1-FO (42-7607) from the 705th Squadron named "The Spirit of 77." It was subsequently converted into a R4-A Radio Counter Measures aircraft.

The I.Jagdkorps formed three Gefechtsverbanden based on JG 3, JG 4, and JG 27. The JG 3 Gefechtsverband hit the 91st Bomb Group of the 1st Bomb Division, shooting down 12 B-17s in a massed attack. They were then attacked by P-51s, losing 51 Fw 190s and Bf 109s, 26 pilots killed and 10 wounded. While trying to recover, a pair of BF 109s of JG 3 tried to land at Borkheide near Berlin. Red flares were fired, attracting the attention of P-51s of the 355th Fighter Group. On the ground were the Bf 109s of I./JG 300 waiting for the scramble order. The P-51s struck the Gruppe before it became airborne, destroying 26 Bf 109 and damaging ten more.

The JG 4 Gefechtsverband was vectored to the off-course 457th Bomb Group, shooting down nine bombers in the initial attack. P-51 fighters arrived and 17 Bf 109s were shot down with 14 pilots killed and six wounded. The JG 27, equipped only with the Bf 109, was hit by Major George Preddy's 328th Fighter Squadron which claimed 25 Bf 109s in the initial engagement. The hapless Geschwader was then hit by other fighters so that by the end of the engagement they had been virtually wiped out, losing 50 Bf 109s, 27 pilots killed and 12 wounded while only claiming six P-51s. Of the 305 Luftwaffe fighters which took part in the fighting, 133 were lost, two-fifths the force. A total of 73 pilots were killed and 32 wounded.

Fighter inspector Adolf Galland had been pressing Berlin to assemble a monster force of 2,500 to 3,000 fighters to conduct "Der Grosse Schlag" (The Great Blow) that would shoot down so many American bombers that it would temporarily halt Eighth Air Force operations over Germany. To build up such a force, Galland urged the senior Luftwaffe commanders to husband their forces. Der Grosse Schlag was expected to happen in mid-November once the force had been assembled.

Any hopes for Der Grosse Schlag were ended on November 6 during a meeting between Hitler and Generalmajor Eckhard Christian, head of the Luftwaffe operations staff. Christian reported to Hitler that of the 52 claimed aerial victories on November 2, 30 were attributed to the 61 Sturmbock fighters and the remaining 22 to the other 244 fighters. With Galland pushing for the Great Blow, Hitler pointed out the obvious flaw in this concept based on these statistics. "If I deploy 2,600 fighters, I can expect to shoot down only 200 (bombers). In other words, the hope of decimating the enemy with a mass employment is not realistic. It is insanity to continue manufacturing aircraft just to give the Luftwaffe a chance to fly around big numbers!"

On learning of the Fuhrer's tirade, Göring ordered all the senior Luftflotte Reich commanders to a conference at the Berlin-Wannsee headquarters the following day for a further dressing-down. Not content with hectoring the senior commanders, recordings of his disdainful three-hour speech were sent around to the fighter Gruppen.

Hitler had other ideas for the fate of Luftflotte Reich. With a major offensive in the Ardennes scheduled within a month's time, Hitler decided to use the reserve of fighters built up for Der Grosse Schlag to support this operation. Luftflotte Reich would transfer most of its units to the command of Luftflotte West to conduct the Führer's "Grosse Schlag," but in the Ardennes rather than in the skies over Germany. On November 20, Hitler informed Luftflotte Reich that all of its Geschwaderen save JG 300 and JG 301 would be subordinated to Luftflotte West for the upcoming offensive.

The dream of new miracle fighters was also evaporating. The Me 163 had a disappointing combat record and was proving unusually deadly to its pilots. On November 7, Galland visited the "Kommando Nowotny" III./JG 6 in Achmer to see the progress of the first Me 262 jet fighter unit. The next day, Eighth Air Force Mission 705 passed over Achmer to bomb the Leuna plant again. I.Jagdkorps decided against intercepting this mission due to the bad weather and poor state of the fighter units in the wake of the November 2 debacle. Nevertheless, the jet Gruppe commander, Major Walter Nowotny, scrambled four of the new fighters to intercept the bombers. Within moments, two of the jets returned to base with technical problems, including Nowotny's own fighter. Nowotny got into the cockpit of a second fighter and led another three fighters to the bomber stream. They were shielded by a handful of Fw 190D-9 fighters conducting air patrols around the base. Oblt. Franz

During a mission to the IG Farben synthetic fuel plant in Blechhammer, Silesia, November 20, 1944, this B-24J commanded by Lt. Col Clarence "Jack" Lokker of the 781st Squadron, 456th Bomb Group suffered a direct hit by Flak between the fuselage and No. 2 engine, leading to a catastrophic disintegration. Surprisingly, six members of the crew managed to escape. Five were captured but Lokker was killed while trying to escape from German soldiers.

Schall claimed one P-51 and two P-47s before being shot down himself. A second Me 262 was also shot down by the escort fighters. Major Nowotny radioed back that his aircraft was on fire, and moments later it crashed about a kilometer away from the Achmer airbase. Galland had been frustrated by the slow pace of the deployment of this new unit, and after the day's grim display, he ordered the Gruppe to stand-down. It was transferred to Lechfeld in Bavaria, further away from roving Allied fighters, in order to undergo more training. It was subsequently redesignated as III./JG 7, discarding the taint of the failed Kommando Nowotny.

The poor weather restricted USAAF Oil Campaign missions until November 20 when 1st Bomb Division conducted an attack on Gelsenkirchen and other synthetic plants in the Ruhr; the Luftwaffe fighter force did not respond. The following day, the Eighth Air Force conducted a major raid on oil targets in central Germany including Leuna. The weather forced the use of H2X radar. The I.Jagdkorps decided to respond and the forces included I./JG 1, III./JG 4 and both JG 300 and JG 301. These totaled about 400 sorties, one of the largest Luftwaffe responses since the summer. This was made possible in part by the large-scale demobilization of Luftwaffe bomber units and the transfer of their pilots to the fighter Gruppen. By mid-October, 20 bomber Gruppen had been disbanded.

In spite of the scale of the Luftwaffe response, the results on November 21 were dismal. The I.JG 1 Gefechtsverband was hit by escort fighters over Gotha-Erfurt, claiming 11 B-17s and two P-51s; this was a significant exaggeration of the actual results. JG 4 claimed one B-17 and a pair of P-51s. JG 300 and JG 301 claimed six escort fighters and a B-17. Actual USAAF losses to the fighters were five B-17s and four P-51s while the other losses were to Flak. Luftwaffe losses again were severe, 61 fighters, 40 pilots killed and 22 wounded. The Eighth Air Force conducted oil missions against Gelsenkirchen on November 23 and against Leuna on November 25 with meek Luftwaffe fighter resistance.

Mission 725 on November 26 was greeted by strong Luftwaffe attacks from I.Jagdkorps on the inbound mission and even by some II.Jagdkorps missions on the egress. A total of 25 USAAF bombers and 6 fighters were shot down. Again, the Luftwaffe suffered a grim toll of 119 fighters lost, 60 pilots killed and 32 wounded. The next day, the Eighth Air Force staged a spoof raid, apparently aimed at Leuna, but consisting solely of escort fighters. I.Jagdkorps ordered a full-scale attack, but once clear of the clouds, JG 1 and JG 3 withdrew when they realized there were no bombers. JG 300 and JG 301 formed a large Gefechtsverband which was attacked by the P-47s and P-51s. The USAAF fighters claimed 98 kills in the air and 4 on the ground for 15 losses of their own. Actual German losses were lower with the Gefechtsverband losing 39 fighters, 27 pilots killed and 8 wounded. While this was taking place, the US heavy bombers conducted a shallow raid against rail targets in southwestern Germany. The II.Jagdkorps tried to intercept but became engaged with the escort fighters losing 19 fighters, 10 pilots killed and 6 wounded. It was another rough day for the Reich defense fighters.

The last major encounter occurred on November 30 when Mission 212 hit the usual assortment of synthetic plants in central Germany including Leuna. The weather was so poor that only JG 300 attempted to intercept, losing four fighters without reaching the bombers.

RAF Bomber Command carried out 11 daylight missions against oil targets in the Ruhr during November, losing 20 bombers, mainly to Flak. These were supplemented by five night-raids, costing 14 bombers to Flak and night-fighters. As in the case of the USAAF raids, the heavy cloud-cover degraded bombing accuracy. Bomber Command by this stage was using both the Oboe and the Gee-H navigation systems which proved useful under the poor autumn weather conditions. The Air Staff on November 3 requested that Bomber Command conduct deep night raids on Leuna and Pölitz to supplement the USAAF attacks. Harris refused on the expectation it would lead to prohibitive losses even though Bomber Command was conducting deep raids against eastern city targets such as Berlin and Stettin. This argument would continue over the next month.

The November Oil Campaign raids were the heaviest to date but had the most disappointing results. The heavy cloud cover forced the USAAF and Bomber Command to rely on radar and navigation aids rather than visual bombing, with the related decrease in accuracy. Shielded by bad weather, German fuel production modestly increased from 316,000 tonnes in October to 337,000 tonnes in November. The bump in November fuel production was also due to the strenuous efforts to rebuild the major plants such as Leuna. An Allied intelligence assessment described the reconstruction of the 11 major synthetic plants in central Germany as "a remarkable recovery." The synthetic plants in the Ruhr that were hit by both Bomber Command and the USAAF were essentially bombed out.

November would prove to be the last gasp of the rebuilding effort and fuel production would continue to decline through the remainder of the war. In spite of its enormous diversion of resources, the Geilenberg Programm, the recovery of the fuel industry failed.

Hitler's December gamble

The Eighth Air Force staged major raids on the synthetic plants in central Germany on December 6 and December 12 but faced no German Luftwaffe fighters. Unknown to the Allies, the German Reich defense force was being held in reserve to support the forthcoming Ardennes offensive. When Operation Autumn Mist hit the First US Army in the Ardennes on December 16, this put a temporary end to Eighth Air Force Oil missions in favor of attacks against German transportation networks in western Germany. Attacks against strategic targets, including oil targets, did not resume until December 31 after the German offensive had been blunted.

Due to the diversion of the Eighth Air Force, the Fifteenth Air Force was tasked with expanding its strikes against the synthetic fuel plants, resulting in its December "Oil Blitz." The remainder of the missions were conducted mainly against railroad marshalling yards. Poor weather limited the missions to three raids in the first two weeks of December, but 19 raids were conducted between December 16 and December 28. The Fifteenth Air Force, a late-comer to Pathfinder tactics, had become very proficient in radar bombing. About 40 percent of its bombs landed within 1,000 feet of the aim point, twice the accuracy of the Eighth Air Force. With only a few exceptions, the

B-17G (42-97069) named "Mon Tete Rouge" (My Red Head), piloted by 2Lt Lawrence Downy Jr., seen here on Mission 283 on March 28, 1944 over France. This aircraft served with the 731st Squadron, 452nd Bomb Group, 1st Bomb Division. Although it survived several of the costliest raids with the luckless 452nd, it was finally shot down by Flak on December 12, 1944 over Kassel, Germany.

December raids encountered very light Luftwaffe fighter attacks. Although Me 163 and Me 262 fighters were observed during missions over Austria and southern Germany, there were few if any attacks.

The first Fifteenth Air Force attack was on December 2 against the Blechhammer and Odertal refineries. On December 8, a "Lone Wolf" mission was conducted at night against the Moosierbaum refinery outside Vienna. These were small scale missions, in this case, only 10 B-24 and 1 B-17. A more conventional mission was staged against oil targets in Germany on December 9, but the poor weather forced about half the bombers to return to base prematurely. Another mission the following day led to a recall of the outbound bombers, once again, due to weather. Weather improved on December 11, leading to a large-scale mission against the Moosierbaum refinery by 120 B-17 and 36 B-24 bombers. The local Flak defenses were described as "accurate and intense." December 12 saw another series of small-scale Lone Wolf missions against Blechhammer and other targets. The Oil Blitz on December 16 involved 96 B-17 and 205 B-24s against the Linz Benzol plant and the Brüx synthetic fuel plant.

Another oil mission on December 17 against Blechhammer and Odertal brought up Luftwaffe fighters in mass for the first and only time in December. The Fw 190s of II.(Sturm)/JG 300 made a rear attack while the Bf 109s of III./JG 300 attacked from the side of the bomber stream. A total of 16 bombers were lost to the attacks, ten of these from the 461st Bomb Group. The P-38 and P-51 escort fighters arrived on the scene moments after the German attack, and JG 300 lost 40 fighters with 20 pilots killed and five wounded. US fighter losses were two P-51s and four P-38s. The improved weather over southern Germany and Austria led to intensification of the Fifteenth Air Force missions against oil targets in Silesia, Austria, and Czechoslovakia. The December Oil Blitz shut down every major refinery and synthetic fuel plant in the Fifteenth Air Force's zone of operation, except for limited production at Moosbierbaum near Vienna. There was very little resistance from the I.Jagdkorps although on occasion German tactical fighter units assigned to the Russian Front conducted small-scale interceptions.

In the face of considerable pressure from senior RAF commanders, Harris finally relented and ordered an oil mission by Bomber Command against the Leuna synthetic

A P-51D (44-11624, code SX-M), piloted by 2Lt. Leroy Pletz of the 352nd Squadron, 353rd Fighter Group, returns to base in Raydon, England after a December 1944 mission. Pletz was credited with destroying three German aircraft and damaging four aircraft by strafing attacks.

plant on the night of December 6–7. A total of 475 Lancasters and 12 Mosquitoes from 1, 3, and 8 Groups took part. Five bombers were lost, primarily to Flak due to the diversion of the shrunken German night-fighter force to another RAF raid on Giessen the same night. The results of the mission were excellent, and photo reconnaissance suggested that production was halted by the raid. As in the case of the USAAF, the German Ardennes offensive diverted many of the Bomber Command missions to transportation targets. The success of the Leuna raid led to a second deep mission on December 21/22 against Pölitz by 207 Lancasters of 5 Group. The mission was not as successful as the Leuna raid, and casualties totaled three Lancasters over Germany and the crash of five Lancasters on returning to England. The losses were due to Flak and there was no Luftwaffe night-fighter activity that night.

A Bomber Command Handley Page Halifax Mk. V under repair in a hangar on December 29, 1944.

On December 6, the Japanese ambassador in Berlin reported to Tokyo that the fuel situation was "clearly Germany's greatest worry." Production in December was down from the November levels since there were no longer any surplus or repair parts to rebuild bombed plants. The planned underground facilities were unlikely to enter production until March at the earliest. This message was decoded by Allied intelligence. On January 15, Speer issued another survey of the fuel situation to Hitler. He noted that December production had fallen behind the slight November increase and that a further dip in January was likely. The stockpile of petrol/gasoline and diesel fuel has been used up and only a small reserve of aviation fuel remained. He had largely given up hope in Flak or fighter defense being able to resist the Allied bombers. He also made it clear to Hitler that the last major import source of petroleum products from Hungary were absolutely vital, especially for the army. The Hungarian supplies of petrol/gasoline and diesel fuel made up about 17 percent of overall German fuel supply, but it made up about 30 percent of army vehicle fuel. Hitler was well aware of this issue, and it was already impacting German strategic planning in the final campaigns of the war.

As mentioned earlier, the attacks on the oil plants also affected other critical chemicals that were produced at the same plants. For example, two plants, Leuna and Oppau, were responsible for three-quarters of German synthetic nitrogen production, vital in the production of ammunition and explosives. Nitrogen production fell from 63,000 tonnes in April 1944 to only 10,300 tonnes in December 1944. The supply of ammonium nitrate for fertilizer was halted in August 1944, and shortages led to the use of extenders in German ammunition as a partial substitute for explosives. The situation became so bad that by late 1944, ammunition was being manufactured with explosives extended with inert fillers such

A formation of P-38J Lightning fighters of the 27th Fighter Squadron, 1st Fighter Group on a mission on December 7, 1944 escorting Fifteenth Air Force bombers to targets in Austria during the December "Oil Blitz." This squadron won the Distinguished Unit Citation for its role in the May 18, 1944 escort mission to Ploesti.

as rock salt. Not surprisingly, this degraded the combat effectiveness of artillery ammunition and other types of munitions. Although the shortage of nitrogen was one of the most obvious results of the Oil Campaign, the shortages covered an extremely wide range of essential chemicals that rippled through various war industries.

The other fuel crisis was coal. The principal fuel for German industry and electrical generation was coal, not liquid fuels. Coal traveled to the industrial regions of the Ruhr, the Saar, and Silesia by rail and barge. The coal supply was vulnerable to disruption of its transportation, especially the Deutsche Reichsbahn railway system and Germany's extensive canal system. The various debates over the target priorities in the autumn of 1944 eventually settled on a compromise, promoted by Air Marshal Tedder. While Tedder paid lip-service to Spaatz's insistence on the Oil Campaign as the first priority, he was able to win Spaatz's support to target German railway marshalling yards, bridges, and other transport targets as the second priority. He also managed to convince Harris to shift the aim points during his city bombing campaign to encompass critical rail yards in the urban areas. Bomber Command played a critical role in demolishing the German industrial canal system since its Lancasters could carry extremely heavy bombs that were ideally suited to damaging canal infrastructure. Heavy bomber missions during the Ardennes campaign in December 1944–January 1945 were heavily directed against transportation targets in western Germany, the heart of German industry.

Bodenplatte

On December 5, senior Luftwaffe fighter commanders attended a briefing by Gen.Maj. Dietrich Peltz, the new commander of II.Jagdkorps at Flammersfeld. Although the commanders anticipated a major operation based on the transfer of so many fighters from Luftflotte Reich to Luftflotte West, this was the first detailed explanation for the operation, codenamed *Bodenplatte* (Base plate). The first phase of the operation consisted of fighter sweeps over the Ardennes aimed at keeping Allied aircraft from intervening in the ground battle. These missions were conducted under poor winter conditions, and there were frequent dog-fights with tactical fighters of the RAF 2 TAF and the USAAF 9th Fighter Command. The air battles reached a crescendo on December 23–25 due to the arrival of a Russian high front that brought clear weather to the Ardennes. In three days of fighting, the Luftwaffe lost 363 fighters; some Gruppen lost half their strength. The air battles on December 17–27 cost the Luftwaffe 644 fighters destroyed, 227 damaged, 354 pilots killed or captured and 133 wounded – all before the main operation.

On December 31, the codewords "Varus-Teutonicus" were broadcast to the Jagdgruppen, warning that the main phase of *Bodenplatte* would start the next morning on New Year's Day. The January 1 mission was intended to catch Allied aircraft on the ground at their forward bases in the Netherlands, Belgium, and France. There was the hope that several hundred or even a thousand might

Operation *Bodenplatte* proved to be extremely costly for Luftflotte Reich when many of its fighters were lost. Here, a Bf 109G is seen in the gun-camera footage of the P-47D of 1Lt. George L Bauer of the 397th Squadron, 386th Fighter Group. Other images in the sequence shows hits on the underbelly fuel tank which appears to be separating in this view, as well as other hits on the fuselage. Bauer was credited with two confirmed kills.

be destroyed. In the subsequent surprise attack by about 850 Luftwaffe aircraft, the Luftwaffe claimed to have destroyed 479 Allied aircraft and damaged 114; subsequent research has reduced this to 232 destroyed and 156 damaged. It was a Pyrrhic victory at best. Luftwaffe losses included 271 fighters destroyed, 65 damaged; 9 Ju 88 night-fighters destroyed and 4 damaged; 213 pilots killed or captured, and 21 pilots wounded. The losses in senior Luftwaffe commanders were particularly severe as many Gruppe and Staffel commanders had to lead the large mass of poorly trained, inexperienced pilots. A total of 22 unit commanders were lost that day. About a half of the fighter losses were due to Allied Flak while about a quarter were due to Allied fighters. About 10 percent were due to German Flak or accidents. *Bodenplatte* was a misuse of the Luftwaffe's beleaguered Reich defense force. A large percentage of the fighter pilots had been trained for aerial combat, and had no experience at all in strafing attacks. *Bodenplatte* gutted many Luftwaffe units and they would not recover in the following months.

January 1945

As a result of the Allied bomber attacks on oil and transportation targets in late 1944, German industry was descending into chaos by January 1945. The industry was starved of supplies of raw materials such as fuel, chemicals, and steel. Even when production did continue, sub-assemblies could not be transported to the main assembly plants, and finished weapons remained trapped in factory yards due to the destruction of the railway networks.

A formation from the 353rd Bomb Squadron, 301st Bomb Group, Fifteenth Air Force transiting over the Alps on their way to targets in southern Germany from their base in Lucera, Italy. The aircraft in the center, B-17G-50-VE 44-8105, is a Pathfinder aircraft fitted with the AN/APS-15 Mickey (H2X) ground radar in place of the usual belly ball turret.

LUFTWAFFE FIGHTER FORCE IN THE WEST, 10 JANUARY 1945								
	Bf 109	Fw 190	Me 163	Me 262	Bf 110	Me 410	Ju 88	He 219
Luftwaffenkommando West								
JG 1	35	56						
JG 2		44						
JG 3	48	24						
JG 4	60	19						
JG 11	31	50						
JG 26	27	82						
JG 53	89							
JG 54		70						
JG 77	52							
Luftflotte Reich								
JG 3	40							
JG 7		14		22				
JG 300	37	99						
JG 301	16	89						
JG 400			19		1			
NJG 1					96			47
NJG 2							108	
NJG 3					40		67	
NJG 4							57	
NJG 5					78		43	
NJG 6					36		67	
NJG 10							14	
NJG 11	52			1			19	
ZG 26		14				39		
Total	487	561	19	23	251	39	375	47

The first major Oil Campaign raid of the New Year took place on January 1 when the Eighth Air Force staged Mission 774 against an assortment of oil and industrial targets. Since the bulk of the German fighter force was part of the *Bodenplatte* operation, Reich defense was left largely to JG 300, JG 301, and a handful of Me 262 fighters of JG 7. JG 301 claimed two bombers, but losses were again severe, totaling 34 fighters, 10 pilots killed and 7 wounded. The poor weather over the next two weeks, plus the demands of the ground campaign, kept the Eighth Air Force attacking transportation targets. When the weather cleared on January 14, a Mission 792 was conducted, with better than average results against synthetic fuel plants due to visual bombing. The weather also led to a heavy commitment by I.Jagdkorps. The JG 301 attack was thwarted by an intervention by escort fighters before they reached the bombers. The JG 300 attacked the isolated 390th Bomb Group that had lagged behind the main bomber stream, claiming 9 B-17s. However, the 357th and 362nd Fighter Squadrons intervened and decimated the German formation, shooting down 56 German fighters with casualties of 35 killed and 7 wounded. Total I.Jagdkorps losses that day were 90 fighters. The Luftwaffe claimed 28 B-17s versus an actual loss of seven bombers along with seven fighters. This air battle marked one of the worst days for the Reich fighter force in terms of pilot casualties. One of the main reasons for the grievous losses was the inadequate training of the new fighter pilots. The few senior pilots referred to the new replacements as Kanonenfutter – Cannon fodder. To make matters worse, JG 301 was transferred for several days from Reich defense to flying fighter-bomber missions against the Red Army, a sure recipe for bloody losses.

Since the Eighth Air Force was heavily involved in supporting ground operations in the Ardennes, the Fifteenth Air Force stepped up its attacks on synthetic fuel plants, especially those in southern German, Silesia, and Czechoslovakia. The sole remaining plant in this area, Moosierbaum near Vienna, was hit with the largest Fifteenth Air Force raid on record, with 1,375 tons dropped on the January 31 mission. The Fifteenth Air Force also resumed small scale raids on oil targets by P-38s in a fighter-bomber role.

Bomber Command conducted a mixture of day and night raids against oil targets, mainly in western Germany. So for example, on the night of January 2–3, 389 bombers hit the

The best of the Luftwaffe single-engine fighters in widespread use in 1944 was the "long-nose" Fw 190D-9. This example, Werk Nr. 601088, was flown by a staff officer of the IV.(Sturm)/JG-3 "Udet" with the Geschwader insignia evident on the nose. It is seen here on display at the National Museum of the US Air Force.

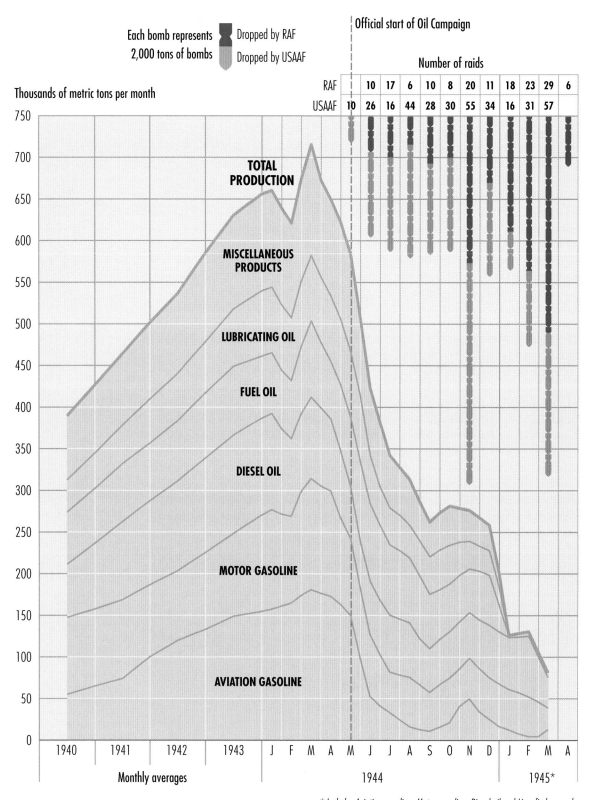

Each bomb represents 2,000 tons of bombs

Dropped by RAF
Dropped by USAAF

Official start of Oil Campaign

Number of raids

RAF		10	17	6	10	8	20	11	18	23	29	6
USAAF	10	26	16	44	28	30	55	34	16	31	57	

Thousands of metric tons per month

TOTAL PRODUCTION

MISCELLANEOUS PRODUCTS

LUBRICATING OIL

FUEL OIL

DIESEL OIL

MOTOR GASOLINE

AVIATION GASOLINE

1940   1941   1942   1943   J F M A M J J A S O N D J F M A

Monthly averages

1944

1945*

* Includes Aviation gasoline, Motor gasoline, Diesel oil and Liquefied gas only

OPPOSITE OIL CAMPAIGN EFFECTS ON GERMAN PETROLEUM PRODUCTION

two I.G. Farben chemical plants in Ludwigshaven while on January 3, a daylight raid was launched against the Benzol plant at Dortmund and the Castrop-Rauxel plant. These missions suffered relatively light casualties. On the night of January 13/14, 5 Group made a deep mission to the synthetic fuel plant at Pölitz and due to the clear conditions, the plant was reduced "to a shambles." The following night a larger force of 573 Lancasters and 14 Mosquitoes hit the Leuna synthetic plant. By this stage, the Leuna plant was only producing a small fraction of its capacity, but Speer later noted that this attack was one of the most destructive of the war. The raid dropped 2,000 tons of bombs on the plant, including 491 4,000 pound blockbusters. Ten Lancasters were lost during the raid, mainly to night-fighters. On the night of January 16/17, three oil targets were hit. The Braunkohle-Benzin synthetic fuel plant at Zeitz was attacked by 328 bombers, with ten Lancasters lost. Another deep raid against Brüx by 231 bombers saw only a single Lancaster lost. The Wanne-Eickel plant was hit by a small force of 138 Lancasters of 3 Group with one aircraft lost. Further raids against oil targets were conducted on the nights of January 22/23 against Duisberg, but weather greatly hampered the January raids.

Luftwaffe demoralization

The morale in the Reich fighter force was undermined by political intrigue by senior Nazi officials. Hitler and Göring had become fed up with Galland's frequent criticisms. In spite of his recent elevation to the rank of Generalleutnant, Galland was pushed out of his role as General der Jadgflieger in favor of a dedicated Nazi, Oberst Gordon Gollob. In response, several senior fighter pilots met in an attempt to bring their complaints directly to Hitler, bypassing the despised Hermann Göring. Göring caught wind of the "mutiny" and called a meeting of senior fighter commanders on January 19. Günther Lützow had commanded 1.Jadgdivision in 1944 before falling out with I.Jagdkorps commander Beppo Schmid. Lützow acted as spokesmen for the other fighter commanders. Their main complaint was the dismissal of Galland who they viewed as an effective and inspiring leader. They charged that Göring's frequent accusations of cowardice directed against the Reich defense pilots were unfair and counterproductive considering their catastrophic loss rate. They also strongly opposed the reorganization of I.Jagdkorps by IX.Fliegerkorps, and especially

To deal with the German jet fighter threat, the Eighth Air Force deployed fighter squadrons to loiter near known German jet bases. The Me 262 was much more vulnerable when it slowed down to land, as seen in this grainy gun camera footage of a Me 262 about to be brought down by an P-47.

B-17G-60-BO "Avengress II" (42-102966 code GD-F) of the 534th Squadron, 381st Bomb Group, during a mission over Germany in early 1945. In this view, its belly turret is retracted suggesting the aircraft is not in the combat zone.

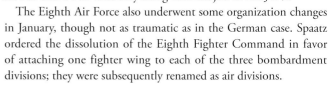

The 392nd Bomb Group conducted five missions against the synthetic fuel plants in the Magdeburg area starting with Mission 817 on February 3, 1945. This B-24J was on the final mission against the Braunkohle Benzin A.G., a synthetic oil refinery, at Rothensee, a suburb of Magdeburg on March 3, 1945.

the role assumed by its new commander, Dietrich Peltz. Peltz was a bomber commander with no experience in Reich defense. Furthermore, he had been a central figure behind the disastrous *Bodenplatte* operation.

In the wake of the "mutiny," Göring exiled Lützow by sending him to command the non-existent fighter force in Italy; Galland was told to take leave far away from Berlin. Eventually, Galland managed to create an improvised Me 262 fighter unit, Jagdverband 44, which attracted many of the surviving top aces. Göring decided to tame the fighter force by replacing most of its senior commanders with more pliable bomber officers.

By late January, the Reich defense force had been greatly reduced by the heavy losses of *Bodenplatte* and the diversion of many surviving groups to the Russian front. Only one full Geschwader, JG 300, was still active over Germany along with the jets of III./JG 7.

The Eighth Air Force also underwent some organization changes in January, though not as traumatic as in the German case. Spaatz ordered the dissolution of the Eighth Fighter Command in favor of attaching one fighter wing to each of the three bombardment divisions; they were subsequently renamed as air divisions.

The Oil Campaign began to have a pronounced impact on Wehrmacht operations. At the start of Operation *Barbarossa* in June 1941, the Wehrmacht, including the *Heer* (army) and Luftwaffe, was consuming about 120,000 barrels (18,000 tons) of fuel per day. By January 1945, its daily fuel consumption had been reduced to 40,000 barrels (6,000 tons) in spite of the fact that the motorized elements of the army had increased three-fold in the same period.

The lack of fuel sapped the army's mobility and distorted German strategic options. For example, when the 6.SS-Panzer-Armee was shifted from the Ardennes to the Russian Front in late January 1945, it was not deployed opposite the Red Army's main Vistula-Oder offensive on the approaches to Berlin. Instead, it was sent to Hungary to reinforce efforts to hold on to the Lake Balaton area. Hungary was the last source of imported oil for Germany, as well as blocking the Red Army from the oil facilities in the Vienna area. Alfred Jodl, chief of Wehrmacht

operations, and Albert Speer later stated that it was fuel shortages in January 1945 that prevented the deployment of a large Panzer reserve of nearly 1,500 tanks to stem the Red Army breakout from the Baranów bridgehead, leading to the loss of Upper Silesia. Upper Silesia was Germany's last industrial stronghold in the east, and shielded Berlin from the final Soviet onslaught.

On January 30, Speer reported to Hitler that the collapse of the fuel industry and transportation network would bring about "the final collapse of the German economy in four to eight weeks… After this, the war can no longer be pursued militarily."

The February decline

The demoralized German fighter force played an increasingly ineffective role in defending against the Allied bomber attacks. Due to the relentless Allied Oil Campaign, only 500 tonnes of aviation fuel were produced in February 1945. Of the 81 major oil targets identified, all 58 refineries were essentially inoperative and only four of the 23 synthetic fuel plants were still producing on a paltry scale.

"The Shack," B-24J-155-CO (44-40298, code Z5-E) of the 754th Squadron, 458th Bomb Group from RAF Horsham St. Faith awaits take-off for its 200th mission, on February 26, 1945. Mission 849 that day was directed against targets in the Berlin area.

Messerschmitt Me 262A-1a (Werk Nr. 112385) at Stendal airbase in April 1945. This was marked as Yellow 8 of JG 7. The Geschwader insignia can be seen below the canopy.

(Note on altitudes: Main Force Bomber Command missions were conducted at an altitude of 7,000–10,000 feet. German night-fighters went out to the rally point over the North Sea at 50 meters/50 yards; and climbed to the same altitude as the bombers during their intruder mission over England.)

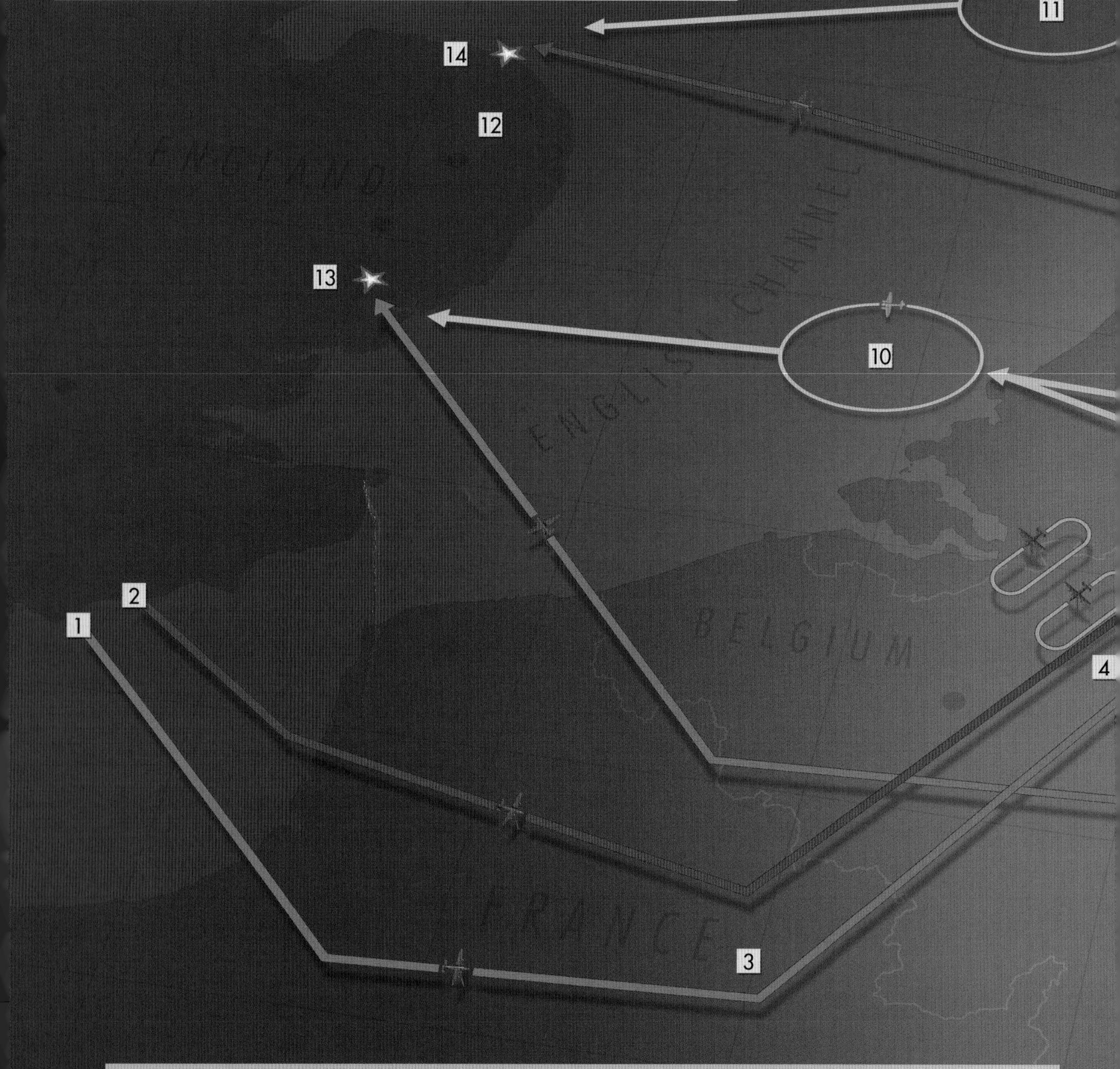

14

12

11

13

10

2

1

BELGIUM

4

3

FRANCE

EVENTS

1 Pathfinder Force of 21 Lancasters and 12 Mosquitoes leads a Main Force of 201 Halifax bombers of 4 Group to attack Bergkamen synthetic fuel plant near Kamen. Formations depart English coast around midnight.

2 5 Group conducts its own mission with its organic Pathfinder elements to attack the Ladbergen aqueduct of the Dortmund-Ems canal that passes over the Mühlenbach river.

3 The two forces approach their targets through northern France where the German radar network has large gaps. Ahead are 91 aircraft of the 100 Group who conduct electronic warfare against the Luftwaffe command-and-control network. Eight Flying Fortresses and Liberators fly alongside the bombers with 214 Squadron using Jostle jammers and 223 Squadron using Piperack radar jammers.

4 Ahead of the Main Force are 16 Halifax of 171 and 199 Squadrons of 100 Group fitted with Mandrel radar jammers. These aircraft fly circular orbits in front of the approaching Main Force to cloak its approach from German radars.

Operation *Gisela*, night of 3–4 March, 1945

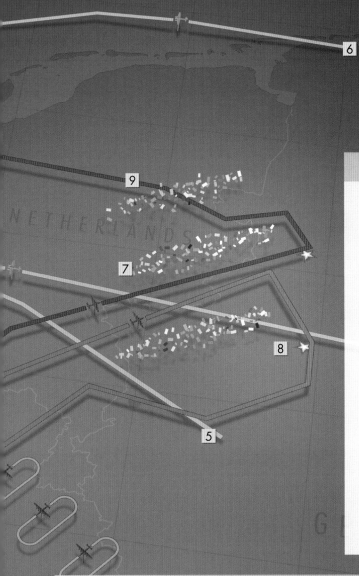

EVENTS

5 The German early warning network along the Dutch coast picks up traces of the British raid before midnight. The IX.Fliegerkorps employ a different approach, conducting intruder operations over Britain after the RAF raid, dubbed Operation *Gisela*. Around midnight, Ju 88 night-fighters of 3.Jagddivision depart their bases in western Germany for the Dutch coast.

6 Ju 88 night-fighters of 2.Jagddivision leave their bases along the northern German coast and fly at about 50 meters off the water once they reach the sea. Some aircraft drop Duppel, to interfere with radar-equipped RAF Mosquito night-fighters prowling in the area.

7 Ahead of the RAF attack, 12 bombers of 100 Group drop large clouds of Window to cloak the approach of the Main Force. 17 other aircraft create a large Window cloud to the north in the Meppen area to create a diversion, and drop Target Indicator flares to enhance the deception.

8 Eight Pathfinder Mosquitoes of 8 Group serve as the vanguard of the Kamen attack, using Oboe navigation aids to mark the Bergkamen synthetic fuel plant. The target is accurately bombed by 4 Group. This force goes unnoticed by the German fighter control posts.

EVENTS

9 Ten Pathfinder Mosquitoes approach the Ladbergen aqueduct and mark the target with red Target Indicators. Lancasters of 9 Squadron lead the attack with 12,000lb Tallboy bombs that shatter the walls of the Dortmund-Ems canal. 5 Group drop 1,000- pounders on the target and put the canal out of operation. German night-fighters shoot down three bombers and Flak bring down two more.

10 The Gefechtsverband of 3.Jagddivision orbit off the Dutch coast through the early hours of March 4.

11 The Gefechtsverband of 2.Jagddivision depart their orbit near the Dutch coast and climb into the RAF bomber stream. The plan is to intercept the RAF bombers over their bases where the crews will be less wary.

12 The 100 Group headquarters in Bylaugh Hall, Norfolk pick up signs of the German *Gisela* mission. Mosquito night-fighters are scrambled to intercept the German intruders. A "scram" warning is issued to returning Bomber Command units.

13 Ju 88 and He 219 night-fighters of 3.Jagddivision begin their operations over Britain starting an hour-long melee. About a hundred German night-fighters attack RAF airfields in Norfolk, Suffolk, Lincolnshire, and Yorkshire. Besides engaging the returning bombers, they shoot down training flights as well as electronic support aircraft of 100 Group.

14 48 RAF aircraft are attacked over England during Operation *Gisela* of which 22 are shot down and eight damaged. Mosquito night-fighters claim five to six German intruders and additional aircraft are lost on the return flight due to damage and crash landings. Operation *Gisela* ends around 0215. It is the last large Luftwaffe offensive mission over Britain of the war.

Göring and Peltz decided to try to make up for the failure of the conventional fighters by expanding the jet fighter force. By late February, JG 7 had three of its Gruppen operational with the Me 262 fighter. A number of former bomber units were scheduled to transition to the jet, starting with I./KG(J) 54. Training by this unit in Germany proved to be hazardous due to roving Allied fighters. Eventually, it was decided to move the fledgling jet units to Austria in the hopes of giving them a haven while completing their operational training. The conversion of bomber units to jet fighter units had mixed results. The bomber pilots were well accustomed to the technical challenges of multi-engine aircraft, but they lacked the aggressive tactical experiences essential for the difficult Reich defense missions.

Allied strategic bomber raids in February frequently met little or no German fighter resistance. Mission 824 on February 9 involved over 1,200 Eighth Air Force bombers and over 800 fighters but was met by only about a hundred Luftwaffe fighters including about two dozen Me 262 jet fighters. The experienced jet fighters of III./JG 7 claimed 4 B-17s and 1 P-51. However, the combat debut of I./KG (J) 54 was not as auspicious, losing five Me 262 fighters including the Gruppe commander who was killed in a collision with a P-51. USAAF losses that day were eight bombers and five fighters while the IX.Fliegerkorps lost nearly a quarter of their force, 21 fighters.

After several small raids, the Eighth Air Force returned in force on February 14, facing significant Luftwaffe resistance for the first time that month. The conventional fighter units conducted 146 sorties and the jets a further 11 sorties. The German fighter attacks were later characterized by American reports as "strikingly weak and almost entirely ineffective" with only a single claim by the conventional fighters. The jets of III./JG 7 claimed 3 B-17 bombers, but the US reported no jet contacts. On February 22, the Eighth Air Force staged Operation *Clarion*, part of a major Allied campaign against German rail and communication junctions. Overall, the German response was feeble except for the jet units. The strengthened JG 7 put up 32 Me 262 fighters and KG (J) 54 a few more, the largest German jet operation so far. The jets claimed two bombers and three fighters but a loss of nine jet fighters. There was no Luftwaffe response to the second day of Clarion operations.

The last major confrontation of the month occurred on February 25 during an Eighth Air Force attack on oil and other targets. This was by far the largest Luftwaffe response of the month with 224 sorties by Bf 109s and Fw 190s and 26 Me 262 jet sorties. Luftwaffe claims were one bomber and two fighters for a loss of 20 fighters including 5 Me 262 jets, mainly from the hapless KG(J) 54.

The Fifteenth Air Force had so effectively smashed the fuel industry in its zone of operation that oil targets in February 1945 were shifted to the small Benzol plants producing vehicle fuel. Three missions were conducted against the Benzol plant in Linz.

RAF Bomber Command continued its night campaign against oil targets, starting with a return mission to the familiar Wanne-Eickel plant on February 2/3, Bottrop and Dortmund on February 3/4 , Gelsenkirchen and Osterfeld on February 4/5. There were occasional daylight raids including an attack on Wanne-Eickel on February 7. The first deep raid of the month was conducted against Pölitz on the night of February 8/9 which essentially put the massive plant out of action for the remainder of the war. There were several further raids on oil targets in the Ruhr area later in the month. Since most of the Ruhr synthetic plants were bombed out, attention shifted to the remaining Bergkamen plant, east of Essen. This led to a surprise Luftwaffe response, dubbed Operation *Gisela,* that attacked the returning RAF bomber force while landing in Britain (*see* Map 2 on pp 82–83).

The final campaign

In the hopes of increasing the lethality of the Me 262 jet fighter against the heavy bombers, the new R4M 55mm rocket was introduced in mid-March 1944. Each fighter could carry

24 of these rockets on two wing racks. The new Ta 152H fighter was deployed with JG 301 in early March. This was a further elaboration of the Fw 190D-9 with better high-altitude performance. It saw its combat debut against the bombers on March 2 with III./JG 301. Fuel supplies were so depleted that the conventional fighters of JG 300 and JG 301 were used mainly to defend the Me 262 jet bases.

Eighth Air Force raids in March 1945 were a mixture of attacks on German railway marshalling yards and oil targets. Although there was ample evidence that the German fuel industry had collapsed, bombing continued to make certain that the plants could not be repaired. The pattern of Luftwaffe actions continued with IX.Fliegerkorps refraining from

A pair of B-24M Liberators of 767th Squadron, 461st Bomb Group, Fifteenth Air Force fly over the island on Drvenik Veliki in Croatia while on the flight back home to their base at Torretto Airfield, Italy after a mission against Mühldorf in Bavaria on March 19, 1945.

To increase the lethality of the Me 262A-1 against bombers, in 1945 it was fitted with a pair of under-wing launch racks for the R4M rocket. The first R4M was tested in February 1945 by Galland's JG 44 and about 60 Me 262s were equipped within a month. These are on a reproduction Me 262A-1 at the Evergreen Aviation & Space Museum. (Creative Commons CC-BY-SA-4.0)

actions on some days, and attempting to defend other targets when fuel supplies permitted. However, the results were usually the same – modest bomber losses versus heavy German fighter losses. For example, on March 2, Mission 859 hit several oil targets including Böhlen and almost two hundred German fighters conducted sorties. They faced over 700 escort fighters. The Luftwaffe claimed 7 B-17s and 1 escort fighter, but lost 53 fighters including 5 Me 262 jets. This was the heaviest engagement of IX.Fliegerkorps during the month of March with subsequent raids usually encountering 50 or fewer German fighters.

The Fifteenth Air Force wrapped up its participation in the Oil campaign in March 1945 due to a lack of worthwhile targets and the advance of the Red Army into its zone of operations. The last mission against the Vienna oil targets took place on March 16. Instead, the Fifteenth Air Force attacked other oil targets in the zone of the Eighth Air Force including two long-range missions against Ruhland, south of Berlin on March 23 and 24. These deep missions near Berlin were resisted by small numbers of Me 262 jet fighters from JG 7.

March was the peak month of Bomber Command raids on German oil targets. By this stage, the synthetic fuel plants had been largely destroyed so the RAF shifted its attention to a variety of minor Benzol plants in western Germany. While the German night-fighter force was increasingly ineffective due to the attrition of crews and the breakdown of the ground-control intercept system, there were some alarming developments. NJG 11 received a single Staffel of Me 262 jet fighters. These were mostly single seat Me 262A, but a few radar-equipped Me 262B arrived. The jet fighters were mainly encouraged to attack Mosquito night-fighters and Pathfinders, which had previously been highly resistant to German night interception due to their speed compared to the Me 110 and Ju 88C.

Overall, about half of Bomber Command raids against oil targets were daylight vs. night raids, 36 vs. 38. The daylight raids often took place in typical winter conditions with heavy cloud cover using the Gee-H navigation aids, and these constituted the majority of the daylight missions, 28 of 36 raids.

The March bomber missions largely finished the destruction of the German oil industry. Aviation fuel production fell from 500 tonnes in February to only 40 tonnes in March and

This B-24M-10-FO, (44-50838) named "Red Bow" of the 714th Squadron, 448th Bomb Group shortly after it was hit in the fuselage by a R4M rocket fired by a Me 262A jet fighter of III./JG 7 on April 2, 1945. Only one crewman managed to escape. The 2nd Division mission that day was to bomb the Parchim airbase where the jet Gruppe was based.

A small number of Me 262B-1a trainers were converted into provisional night-fighters with the FuG 218 Neptun radar. This aircraft (Werk Nr. 110305) was flown operationally by Oberrleutnant Kurt Welter of the only jet night-fighter Staffel, 10./NJG 11. This particular aircraft was surrendered to the British army at Schleswig in May 1945 and is seen here after British markings were applied prior to transfer to the UK. It is currently preserved at the South African National Museum of Military History in Johannesburg.

none at all in April. To put this in some perspective, a Me 262 sortie required about 1.5 tonnes of fuel, so the total March production would have provided enough for only about two dozen flights.

The situation had become so desperate that the Luftwaffe began to consider ramming attacks as a viable tactic to stop the USAAF raids. The special *Sonderkommando Elbe* was formed using modified Bf 109 fighters without armament, radio, and other extraneous equipment. A call for volunteers among novice pilots was issued in March, with some skeptical Luftwaffe commanders limiting the cadre to 200 pilots. The formation was ready by April 1945 and first committed to action as Operation *Werwolf* on April 7 against Mission 931, an Eighth Air Force attack on a mixture of railway and oil targets. Of the 188 modified Bf 109s

A formation of B-24J bombers of the 788th Squadron, 467th Bomb Group, 2nd Division during Mission 962 against Zwiesel on April 20, 1945. The smoke is from a special marker dropped by the lead bombardier as a visual cue for the other bombers to release their bomb-load.

available, 143 sortied, but many had to return before reaching the bombers due to equipment malfunctions. A total of 14 bombers were knocked down by the ramming attacks and another seven were so badly damaged that they crash-landed at forward bases or were scrapped after returning to Britain. The Sonderkommando Elbe lost 45 fighters along with 32 pilots killed or captured and five wounded. USAAF losses that day totaled 17 bombers, mainly to ramming attacks, with Me 262 fighters claiming six bombers and three escort fighters. The proponents of the *Werwolf* tactics optimistically expected to inflict such heavy losses that it would lead to a reduction in USAAF bomber attacks. Although the April 7 casualties were the highest since early February 1945, they were not unusually severe compared to many 1944 missions. Sonderkommando Elbe was subsequently disbanded due to its unimpressive results, and the disgust that many senior Luftwaffe commanders felt about such grotesque tactics.

The growing role of the Me 262 in bomber interception led to a special raid by the Eighth Air Force on April 10 when Mission 938 was dispatched to attack a German headquarters at Oranienburg plus a number of airfields suspected of use as jet fighter bases. The Luftwaffe response consisted of about 60 Me 262 fighter sorties, a single Me 163 rocket fighter, and four of the new Ta 152H fighters. The jets claimed to have shot down 16 bombers and ten escort fighters. In the process, the Luftwaffe units lost about 15 Me 262 jet fighters in the air, plus numerous aircraft destroyed on the ground due to the bombing. By this stage of the campaign, the Me 163 was no longer operational on a regular basis and the April 10 mission appears to have been a test of the new Jägerfaust, an array of ten 50mm weapons aimed vertically and triggered automatically by a photocell. This fighter claimed to have shot down a B-17 or Lancaster bomber on the mission. By April 1945, there was no longer a German fuel industry worth defending.

Me 262A-1a of JV 44 at its final base at Innsbruck-Hötting in the Austrian Alps in late April 1945. JV 44 was led by Adolf Galland and contained a high proportion of top Luftwaffe aces. Behind it is a Ju 87D-3 Stuka (E8+GL) night-bomber of NSG 9.

ANALYSIS

The Oil Campaign was amongst the most decisive air campaigns of World War II. Speer later noted that "As a result of the losses in the fuel industry, it was no longer possible even in December 1944 and January 1945 to make combat use of the decreased armaments production. The loss of fuel, in my opinion, had a more decisive effect on the outcome of the war than the hardships with armaments and transport."

By early 1945, fuel shortages had crippled large segments of the German armed forces, and profoundly limited the operational capabilities of the rest. Nearly all of the Luftwaffe

One of the final "miracle aircraft" to appear in 1945 was the Heinkel He 162 Volksjäger. A handful reached unit service in the final days of the war. This example was found at the Junkers Zweigwerk in Bernburg, and was the 27th of 29 He 162 fighters built there before the plant was captured by the US Army in mid-April 1945.

Me 163B-1a Werk Nr. 191301, on display at the Udvar-Hazy Center of the National Air and Space Museum outside Washington DC. This aircraft was one of five of these rocket fighters brought back to the US for evaluation. It has been conserved in what remains of its original markings and colors though some spot re-painting was probably done over the years.

formations except for select fighter units were grounded. Even the elite units such as the Me 262 fighters had their operations severely curtailed by lack of fuel. U-Boat operations were restricted by fuel shortages and surface warships had been left in port since the autumn of 1944. The German army was forced to use horse traction for much of its tactical logistics since liquid fuel was simply not available.

The Oil Campaign absorbed a relatively small fraction of the overall Allied strategic bombing effort. Of the 1.5 million tons of bombs dropped by the strategic bomber forces, only about 15.9 percent was assigned to the Oil Campaign compared to 27.5 percent to area bombing of German cities, mainly by RAF Bomber Command. The remainder was devoted to raids on German industry, German transportation targets, and tactical support of the ground campaign.

BOMB TONNAGE DURING OIL CAMPAIGN 1944–45*								
	Eighth AF		Fifteenth AF		RAF Bomber Command		Overall Total	
	No. of Attacks	Tonnage of Bombs	No. of Attacks	Tonnage of Bombs	No. of Attacks	Tonnage of Bombs	Total tons	% of CBO missions
May 1944	11	2,883	10	1,540	—	—	4,423	5.37
June	20	3,689	32	5,653	10	4,562	13,904	12.0
July	9	5,379	36	9,313	20	3,829	18,521	16.2
August	33	7,116	23	3,997	20	1,856	12,969	18.3
September	23	7,495	8	1,829	14	4,488	13,812	11.6
October	18	4,462	10	2,515	10	4,088	11,065	11.3
November	32	15,884	19	4,168	22	16,029	36,081	31.0
December	7	2,937	33	6,226	15	5,722	14,885	14.4
January 1945	17	3,537	5	2,023	23	10,114	15,674	20.2
February	20	6,161	20	4,362	24	15,749	26,272	20.6
March	36	9,550	24	6,628	33	21,211	37,389	21.5
April	7	1,949	1	124	9	5,993	8,066	6.3
Totals	233	71,042	221	48,378	200	93,641	213,061	12.1%

Tonnage= Short tons (2,000 lb)

	TONNAGE ON OIL TARGETS	PERCENTAGE OF CBO ON OIL TARGETS
Pre-May 1944	5,670	1.1
May 1944	5,571	5.37
June	17,033	12.0
July	22,831	16.2
August	26,484	18.3
September	13,585	11.6
October	13,950	11.3
November	35,558	31.0
December	15,779	14.4
January 1945	15,891	20.2
February	24,427	20.6
March	36,690	21.5
April	7,007	6.3
Total	240,476	12.1
Total RAF	102,615*	
Total USAAF	137,861	

An important but often overlooked aspect of the Oil Campaign was its devastating effect on other critical industrial products including explosives. Since the German chemical industry was highly integrated, the destruction of major chemical plants such as the Leuna plant also resulted in crippling production of chemical products beyond synthetic fuel.

The importance of the Oil Campaign led the Allies to undertake a substantial study of the results of the bombing. Overall, the most significant tactical finding was the difficulty in destroying industrial targets. This was due in part to the poor accuracy of World War II bombers. A study of three of the main plants, Leuna, Ludwigshafen-Oppau, and Zeitz, disclosed that of 30,000 tons of bombs dropped on these plants, only 3,781 tons of bombs actually struck within the confines of the plants. Daylight bombing in good visibility offered the best results. The table below summarizes the results.

BOMBING ACCURACY DURING OIL CAMPAIGN		
Formation	Aiming technique	Percentage of hits inside the plant
USAAF Eighth Air Force	visual aiming	26.8
RAF Bomber Command	night, Pathfinder	15.8
USAAF Eighth Air Force	H2X radar	5.4

Not only was bombing accuracy rather poor, but German records indicated that 14.1 percent of the bombs that did strike within the plant ground failed to explode due to faulty fuzes or bombs landing flat due to fin damage. Of the bombs that fell within the plant grounds, only about 3 percent actually struck a building or major piece of equipment. However, even those bombs that did not strike a building were often destructive in other ways. These plants depended very heavily on the input of outside sources of electrical power, water, and transport lines. Bomb damage against electrical and water supply halted production as effectively as hits on critical industrial equipment. Disruption of rail transport in and around the factories prevented shipment of completed product from the plant. During the first two USAAF raids on Leuna, 94 percent of the utilities had to be repaired before production could be resumed. Through November 1944, there were 1,500 breaks in the water system feeding the Leuna facility and a total of 5,000 breaks in various utilities. This level of infrastructure damage

By February 1945, the German synthetic fuel industry had been largely destroyed. This is the IG Farben plant in Ludwigshafen, a sophisticated chemical plant that produced synthetic fuel, Buna artificial rubber, plastics, and a variety of other products.

reduced Leuna's productive capacity to only about 9 percent of that obtained prior to the start of the campaign in May 1944.

The types of bombs used in the Oil Campaign had varied results. The most effective bombs were the very heavy 2,000–4,000lb bombs dropped by RAF Lancasters. Many plants had vital structures protected by concrete blast walls. The heavy RAF bombs were the only bombs powerful enough to demolish these walls; the 500lb bombs typical of USAAF raids were not as effective short of a direct hit. Incendiary bombs were not as effective as might be expected since the German fire services were often able to extinguish them before they made contact with inflammable chemicals.

German active defenses such as Flak and fighters caused significant Allied losses, but failed to stem the Allied bomber onslaught. Bomber casualties were actually lighter in USAAF day-light raids than RAF night raids. The USAAF figures varied depending on the location of the target. Those located in eastern Germany, Poland, and Czechoslovakia tended to be higher than those in western German since the bombers could be subjected to more prolonged attacks by fighters. Overall, the Luftwaffe was increasingly ineffective in intercepting the Eighth Air Force bomber missions. On average the Eighth Air Force lost 3.2 percent of its bomber force per mission in 1944, while losses in 1945 shrank to 1.0 percent. RAF losses during night-time raids in the early summer of 1944 were significantly higher, often well over 5 percent, due to the German night-fighter force. These figures began to decline later in the summer, in part due to advances in electronic warfare tactics that undermined German technology.

QUARTERLY LOSSES OF LUFTWAFFE SINGLE ENGINE FIGHTERS IN 1944					
	To 31 Mar	to 30 Jun	to 30 Sep	to 31 Dec	Annual total
Quarterly losses					
West	2,700	3,569	4,231	3,560	14,060
East	391	511	705	496	2,103
Total	3,091	4,080	4,936	4,056	16,163

The "wonder weapons" deployed in 1944–45 were unable to stem Germany's decline. The Me 163 was largely ineffective due to its dangerous propulsion system. The Me 262 was a revolution in fighter performance, but its lack of engine durability and growing production quality problems meant that only a handful of jet fighters were available at any one time.

The Luftwaffe generally regarded the Flak performance to be disappointing in the second half of 1944 in view of the small number of bombers actually shot down compared to the enormous resoures poured into the Flak force. American commanders had a somewhat different view of the Flak threat, recognizing the small numbers of bomber losses attributable to Flak alone, but more aware of the significant number of stragglers damaged by Flak and then shot-down by fighters. Furthermore, Flak intimidated bomber crews and played a crucial role in degrading bomber accuracy. Flak accounted for about 26 percent of the Eighth Air Force bombers shot down in 1943 and 36.5 percent in 1944.

German fighters had been the predominant cause of bomber losses to enemy action in 1944, accounting for 63.5 percent of the USAAF losses compared to 36.5 by Flak. In contrast, during 1945 German fighters accounted for 55 percent of Eighth Air Force bombers losses and 45 percent to Flak due to the weakened Luftwaffe fighter force.

German passive defenses were marginally successful. Decoy plants were a problem for USAAF daylight missions. During the first seven major attacks on the Leuna complex, nearly as many tons of bombs were dropped on the decoy plant as on the actual facility. The widespread use of smoke generators to hide the plants largely depended on weather conditions. In the right conditions, the smoke was effective in degrading the accuracy of USAAF daylight missions. However, the wind was not always cooperative and, on many days, the smoke was dispersed.

FURTHER READING

Government Studies

US Strategic Bombing Survey Reports

Aircraft Division Industry Report, (No. 4, Aircraft Division)

Oil Division Final Report, (Oil Division)

The Defeat of the German Air Force, (No. 59, Military Analysis Division)

The Effects of Strategic Bombing on the German War Economy, (No. 3, Office of the Chairman)

US Air Force Historical Studies (Maxwell Air Force Base)

Stephen Fraley, *Electronic Combat over the Third Reich*, (Air Command and Staff College, 1988)

Walter Grabmann, *German Air Force Air Defense Operations*, (No. 164, 1956).

Waldo Heinrichs, *A History of the VIII USAAF Fighter Command*, (n.d.)

Josef Kammhuber, *Problems in the Conduct of a Day and Night Defensive Air War*, (No. 179, 1953).

Josef Schmid, *The German Air Force versus the Allies in the West: German Air Defense*, (No. 159, 1954).

Josef Schmid and Walter Grabmann, *The German Air Force versus the Allies in the West: The Air War in the West*, (No. 158, 1954).

Richard Suchenwirth, *Command and Leadership in the German Air Force*, (No. 174, 1969).

Scott Wuesthoff, *The Utility of Targeting the Petroleum-Based Sector of a Nation's Economic Infrastructure*, (Air University Press, 1994)

n.a., *Ultra and the History of the United States Strategic Air Force in Europe vs. the German Air Force*, September 1945.

Books

Dieter-Theodor Bohlmann, *Sokrates: Reichsluftverteidigung im Stader Land*, Kreissparkkasse, Stade: 2009

Horst Boog, et. al., *Germany and the Second World War 1944, Vol VII*, Oxford University Press, Oxford: 2006

Horst Boog, et. al., *Das Deutsche Reich und der Zweite Weltkrieg 1945*, Band 10, DVA, Munich: 2008

Donald Caldwell, *Day Fighters in Defence of the Reich: A War Diary 1942–45*, Frontline, Barnsley: 2011

Donald Caldwell and Richard Muller, *The Luftwaffe over Germany: Defense of the Reich*, Greenhill, London: 2007

Ronald Cooke, Roy Nesbit, *Target: Hitler's Oil, The Allied Attacks on German Oil Supplies 1939–45*, William Kimber, London: 1985

Sebastian Cox (ed.), *The Strategic Air War against Germany 1939–45*, Frank Cass, London: 1998

W. F. Craven & J. L. Cate, *The Army Air Forces in World War II, Vol. 3 Europe – Argument to VE Day*, University of Chicago, Chicago: 1951

Richard Davis, *Carl Spaatz and the Air War in Europe*, Center for Air Force History, Washington DC: 1983

Robert Ehlers, *Targeting the Third Reich: Allied Intelligence and the Allied Bombing Campaigns*, University Press of Kansas, Lawrence: 2009

Dietrich Eichholtz, *War for Oil: The Nazi Quest for an Oil Empire*, Potomac Books, Dulles, VA: 2012

Roger Freeman, *The Mighty Eighth: A History of the US 8th Army Air Force*, Doubleday, New York: 1970

Roger Freeman, *The Mighty Eighth War Diary*, Arms & Armour, London: 1981

Roger Freeman, *The Mighty Eighth War Manual*, Arms & Armour, London: 1984

Werner Gerbig, *Die Luftoffensive gegen die deutsche Treibstoffindustrie und der Abwehreinsatz 1944–1945*, Motorbuch, Stuttgart: 2003

F.H. Hinsley, et al, *British Intelligence in the Second World War, Vol.3, Parts 1 and 2*, HMSO, London: 1988

David Isby ed., *Fighting the Bombers: The Luftwaffe's Struggle against the Allied Bomber Offensive*, Greenhill, London: 2003

Peter Kaššák & David Gunby, *Gardening by Moonlight: 205 Group RAF Mining Operations over River Danube in 1944*, Degart, Bratislava: 2017

Kevin Mahoney, *Fifteenth Air Force against the Axis: Combat Missions over Europe during World War II*, Scarecrow, Lanham, MD: 2013

John Manrho and Ron Pütz, *Bodenplatte: The Luftwaffe's Last Hope*, Hikoki, Mardens Hill: 2004

Charles McArthur, *Operations Analysis in the US Army Eighth Air Force in World War II*, American Mathematical Society, Providence: 1985

Stephen McFarland & Wesley Newton, *To Command the Sky: The Battle for Air Superiority over Germany 1942–44*, Smithsonian, Washington DC: 1991

Martin Middlebrook & Chris Everitt, *The Bomber Command War Diaries*, Pen & Sword, Barnsley: 2020

Arthur Mierzejewski, *The Collapse of the German War Economy 1944–1945*, U. of N. Carolina, Chapel Hill: 1988

Williamson Murray, *Strategy for Defeat: The Luftwaffe 1933–45*, Air University Press, Huntsville: 1983

Alfred Price, *Battle over the Reich*, Ian Allen, London: 1973

Alfred Price, *Battle over the Reich: The Strategic Bomber Offensive over Germany, Volume Two 1943–45*, Ian Allen, London: 2005

Alfred Price, *The History of US Electronic Warfare, Volume 1: The Years of Innovation – Beginning to 1946*, Association of Old Crows, Washington DC: 1984

Martin Streetly, *Confound & Destroy: 100 Group and the Bomber Support Campaign*, Jane's, London: 1978

M. Svejgaard, *Der Luftnachrichten Dienst in Denmark*, Gyges, Copenhagen: 2003

Arthur Tedder, *With Prejudice: The World War II Memoirs of Marshal of the RAF Tedder*, Little, Brown, New York: 1966

John Verbeek & Kees Neisingh, *German Radar in the Netherlands*, Boek Press, Soest: 2021

Randall Wakelam, *The Science of Bombing: Operational Research in RAF Bomber Command*, U. of Toronto, Toronto: 2009

Charles Webster and Noble Frankland, *The Strategic Air Offensive against Germany 1939–1945*, Vols. 3 & 4, HMSO, London: 1961

Edward Westermann, *Flak: German Anti-Aircraft Defenses 1914–45*, University Press of Kansas, Lawrence: 2001

INDEX

Page numbers in **bold** refer to illustrations. Some caption locators are in brackets. *Italic* page numbers refer to tables.

air defenses 13–14, **15** (14), **16**, **18**, 21–22
see also Flak defenses
Air Ministry 4, 5, 30
aircraft 43
  "ace-on-ace" fighter duels 33
  B-17 **9**, **11**, 17, 46, 50, 63, 72, 77
  B-17G **47**, **51**, **52**, **53**, **61**, **71**, **76**
  B-24 32, **38**, 46, 50, 53, **60**, 63, 65, 72
  B-24H **12**, **68**
  B-24J **30**, **37**, **66**, **69**, **80**, **81**, **87**
  B-24M **85**, **86**
  B17G-60-BO **80**
  Bf 109 12, 17, 32, 33, 38, 46, 50, 63, 68, 72, 87–88
  Bf 109 G **75**
  Bf 109 G-14 **21**
  Bf 110G-4 **44**
  engines 18–19
  fighter/bomber confrontations 32–33
  Fw 190 12, 32, 63, 72
  Fw 190A 17, **20**, 50
  Fw 190D-9 **14**, 69, **77**, 85
  Fw190F-8 **13**
  Halifax Bomber 7, **8**, 42, 45, 53, **63**, **64**, **65**, 66, **73**
  He 162 Volksjäger **89**
  He 219 Uhu 42
  insignia **81**
  jet and rocket fighters 18–19
  Ju 87D-3 Stuka **88**
  Ju 88G **13**, **21**, 44
  Lancaster Bomber 7, **41**, 42–43, **43**, 44–45, 64, 66, **67**, 73, 74, 79, 92
  Me 163 Komet 18, **48–49** (47), 51–52, 61, 63, 69, 72, 88, 92
  Me 163B-1 a **89**
  Me 262 5, 18–19, 62–63, 65, 67, 69, 72, 77, **79**, **81**, 84–85, 87–88, **87**, **88**, 92
  Me 410 17, 46, 50, **58–59** (57), 62
  Me 410B **32**
  Mosquito Bomber 7, 8, **8**, 9, 22, 42–43, 44, 45, 64, 73, 79
  P-38 **4**, 33, 52, **55**, 63, 72
  P-38H-5 **4**
  P-38J **74**
  P-47D Thunderbolt 11, **12**, 32, 33, **56**, 70

P-51B **62**
P-51D Mustang 11, **12**, 38, 46, **46**, 50, 64, 68, 70, 72, **72**
  production *19*
Spitfire 45, 64
Ta 152H 85, 88
Tempest 64
Wellington Bomber 53
Wellington Mk. X **28–29** (27)
Zerstörer heavy fighters 17
Ardennes 71, 73, 74–75
Auschwitz **52**

"Battle opera houses" 14, **16**
bombing raids 4, 25, **26**, 27, 31, 31–36, **31**, **34–35**, 37–39, **37**, 41–45
  accuracy 91, *91*
  altitude **82–83**
  Blechhammer and Odertal refineries 72
  bomb tonnage 90, *90*
  bomb types 92
  Bottrop raid 44–45
  cloud cover 60, 67
  daylight missions 11, 86, 91
  heavy bomber missions *45*
  Gelsenkirchen raids 41–42, 70
  Homberg raid 44–45
  IG Farben **52**, **61**, 77, 79, **91**
  infrastructure damage 91–92, **91**
  Leuna plant 5, 18, 33, **48–49** (47), 50, 51, 63, 67, 69, 70, 71, 72–73, 79, 91–92
  Lone Wolf missions 72
  Mission 353 31–36, **34–35**
  Mission 421 45–46
  Mission 425 46
  Mission 438 47
  Mission 447 47
  Mission 458 47, 50
  Mission 484 50
  Mission 501 50
  Missions 514, 519, 524 and 556 51–52
  Missions 568 and 570 **51**, 52
  Mission 623 60–61, **62**
  Mission 626 61–62
  Missions 650 and 652 63
  Mission 669 65
  Missions 696 and 698 67
  Mission 705 69
  Mission 725 70
  Missions 744 and 792 77
  Mission 824 84
  Mission 859 86

  Mission 931 87–88
  Mission 938 88
  night bombing 7, **11**, **82–83**
  Ploesti raids 4, 25, 27, 30, 37–39, **37**, 52–55, *54*
  radar-directed bombing 67, 71–72
  Ruhr area 66, 67, 70
  Scholven Buer 43, 44
  spoof raids 70
  Wesseling raid 42–43, 44
"The Bottisham Four" **46**
Breves, Hptm Adolf 42
"Bungay Buckaroos" **68**

capabilities
  attackers 7–12
  defenders 13–24
casualties and losses 5, 17, 18, 32, 36, 38, 39, 42, 43, 44–45, 46, 50, 51–52, 53, 61–62, 63, 65, 68, 70, 75, 77, 79, 86, 88, 92, *92*
  point scoring fighter claims 32, 33
chaff *see* Window
Christian, GenMaj Eckhard 68–69
Churchill, Winston 30, 39, 41, 63

data collection and dissemination 14
Der Grosse Schlag (The Great Blow) 68–69
dogfights 75

Eisenhower, Gen. Dwight D. 27, 30, 60
electronic warfare 9, **10**, 14, **16**, 22, 43–44

FAAR (Royal Romanian Air Force) 53
Flak defenses 4–5, 9, 14, 22, **22**, **23**, 24, **25**, 33, 41, 46, 50, **51**, 53, **69**, 75
  effectiveness 92
fuel supplies
  coal 74
  and explosives manufacture 56, 73–74, 91
  exports from Romania *54*
  German reduction in operational flight activity 55–56
  production 39–41, 50, 54, 55, 64, 71, 73, **78** (79), 81, 86–87
  shortages 5, 19, 36, 39, 55–56, 57, 80, 89–90
  transport 41
  underground production facilities 40–41, **40**, 73
  vulnerability 25, 27

Galland, Adolf 36, 50, 68, 69, 70, 79, 80
"Gardening" missions **28–29** (27), 30
Geilenberg, Edmund 40–41, 71
Gollob, Obst Gordon 79
Göring, Hermann 36, 62, 69, 79–80, 84
ground control-interception 9, 14, **16**, **18**, 21

Harris, AM Arthur "Bomber" 4, 5, 7, 30, 41, 63, 64, 66–67, 70, 72, 74
Himmelbelt system 13
Hitler, Adolf 2, 39, 55, 56, 64, 68–69, 73, 79, 81
"Horst Wessel" **58–59** (57)
Hungary 25, 53–54, **53**, 80–81

intelligence 4, 9, 11, 14, 36, 39, 41, 71

Jodl, Alfred 80–81
Joint Intelligence Committee 39

Kammhuber line 13
Karin Hall plan 25
Kogler, ObstLt Hans 20–21
Kriegsmarine 36, 56, 90

Luftwaffe 4–5, 25, 53, *54*, 89–90
    daylight tactics 19–21
    and defense of the Reich 13–14, **15** (14), 21–22, 56–57, 69, 71, 77
    demobilization of bomber units 70
    demoralization 79–81
    fighter force 16, *17*
    fighter force in the west *76*
    ground control-interception system 9, 14, **16**, **18**, 21
    jet fighter force 84
    night tactics 21–22, 42–45
    order of battle *24*
    organization 13–19, **15**, 36, 79–80, 84
    shadow units 14
    Sonderkommando Elbe 87–88
Lützow, Günther 79, 80

Modrow, Hptm Ernst-Wilhelm 42, 43
morale 79–81
Müller, ObstLt Friedric-Karl "Tutti" 32, 39

navigation 7–8, 12, 42, 70
Nowotny, Maj Walter 69–70

Oberkommando Luftwaffe (OKL) 55–56
oil campaign
    analysis 89–92
    August campaign, assessment of 55–57
    Bodenplatte 74–75, **75**, 77, 80
    bomb tonnage 90, *90*
    Bomber Command involvement 41–45, 70–71, 72–73, 77, 79, **82–83**, 84, 86

chronology 6
collapsing the German war economy 31–36
events of August 1944 51–52
events of December 1944 71–74
events of February 1945 81, 84
events of January 1945 75, 77, 79
events of November 1944 67–71, **68**
Fall 1944 campaign 60
final stages of 84–88
German countermeasures 39–41
heavy bomber missions *45*
initial campaign, impact of 39
objectives 25–30, **26**
October 1944 missions 65–67, **66**
petroleum production, effects on **78** (79)
Ploesti attacks 37–39, **37**, 52–55, *54*
post-invasion USSTAF campaign 45–51
Operation *Argument* 11
Operation *Autumn Mist* 71
Operation *Barbarossa* 80
Operation *Bodenplatte* 74–75, **75**
Operation *Clarion* 84
Operation *Crossbow* 4, 30
Operation *Gisela* **82–83**, 84
Operation *Market-Garden* 60
Operation *Overlord* 4, 27, 45
Operation *Pointblank* 11, 12, 20, 27, 36
Operation *Tidal Wave* 25, 27
Operation *Werwolf* 87

Pathfinder 7–9, 22, 42, 46, 47, 60, **76**, **82–83**
Peltz, GenMaj Dietrich 74, 80, 84
pilots 5, 52, 84
    quality of 57
    training 12, 19, 36, 57, 77
Pletz, 2Lt Leroy **72**
Portal AM Charles 4, 30, 63, 67

radar 8, 9, 12, 14, **18**, **21**, 32, 43–44, 56, 60, **76**
    detectors 22
    jammers 9, 12, 14, 21, 44
    radar-directed bombing 67, 71–72
radio communications 9, 14
railways 41, 60, **60**, 71, 74, 75, 85, 91
Rall, Maj Gunther 33
Romania 25, 27, 30
Rotterdam Commission 22
Royal Air Force 21, 25, 27, 92
    100 Group 9, 21, 44, **82–83**
    205 Group 30, **38**
    Bomber Command 4, 5, 7, 39, 41–45, *45*, 66, 70–71, 72–73, 77, 79, **82–83**, 84, 86
    capabilities 7–11
    oil campaign missions 63–64, 66–67

and Pathfinder 7–9, 22, 42, 46, 47, 60, **76**, **82–83**

Schmid, Beppo 36, 79
Schmid, GenMaj Josef 31
Schnaufer, Hptm Heinz-Wolfgang 42, 43
Schubert, Fw. Siegfried 47, 52, 65
searchlights **19**, 21
smoke dischargers and markers 37, **37**, **87**, 92
Spaatz, Gen. Carl 4, 27, 30, 36, 41, 53, 74, 80
Speer, Albert 33, 36, 39–40, 55, 56, 64, 73, 79, 81, 89
Sperrle, GFM Hugo 19
Sterkrade-Holten raid 42
Stumpff, GenObst Hans-Jürgen 31

tactics
    *Gardening" missions **28–29** (27), 30
    escort tactics 31
    Luftwaffe daylight tactics 19–21
    Luftwaffe night tactics 21–22
    mass attacks 20–21
    ramming attacks 87–88
    Wilde Sau (Wild Boar) tactics 22, 31
target flares 8–9
Tedder, AM Arthur 4, 27, 63, 66, 74
Transportation Plan 27, 30

United States Strategic Air Force (USSTAF) 25, 27, 92
    capabilities 11–12
    Eighth Air Force 4, 11–12, 30, 31, 38–39, 45, 60, 61–62, 63, 65, 66, 67, 70, 71, 77, 80, 84, 85, 92
    Fifteenth Air Force 4, 11, 30, 37, **37**, 39, 53–54, **53**, *54*, **66**, 67, 71–72, 77, 84, 86
    post-invasion oil campaign

weapons
    bombs **41**, 90, *90*, 91, *91*, 92
    cannon 17, **20**, 50, **58–59** (57)
    explosives manufacturing 56, 73–74, 91
    GB-1 guided bomb 32
    Jägerfaust 88
    machine guns **11**, 17, **20**
    mines **28–29** (27)
    rockets 5, 17–18, 19–20, **48–49** (47), 51–52, 67, 84–85, **85**, **86**
    see also Flak defenses
weather conditions 30, 31, 37, 42, 46, 47, 60, 65, 67, 70–71, 72, 77
Wehrmacht 5, 16, 27, 36, 39, *54*, 56, 80–81, 90
Window 9, 12, 14, 21, 43, 44, **82–83**

Zemke, Col. Hub 33